THE PHILOSOPHY OF INTEGRATING MEDICAL ANTHROPOLOGY & CLINICAL PSYCHOLOGY: MENTAL HEALTH & SOUL HEALTH

A QUEST FOR SOLUTIONS TO HUMAN HEALTH, DISEASES, TREATMENT AND PREVENTION

DR. SABELO SAM GASELA MHLANGA

WESTBOW
PRESS®
A DIVISION OF THOMAS NELSON
& ZONDERVAN

WestBow Press books may be ordered through booksellers or by contacting:

WestBow Press
A Division of Thomas Nelson & Zondervan
1663 Liberty Drive
Bloomington, IN 47403
www.westbowpress.com
844-714-3454

ISBN: 978-1-6642-9737-1 (sc)
ISBN: 978-1-6642-9736-4 (e)

Print information available on the last page.

WestBow Press rev. date: 04/25/2023

CONTENTS

PREFACE

Medical Anthropology is the study of human health, disease, treatment, prevention, and health care system. This includes the scientific study of humanity, human behavior, human biology, culture, linguistics, and societies, in the past, present, and future. Medical Anthropology investigates and examines people's health and illness in the context of understanding their bodies and souls. Medical Anthropology draws upon social, cultural, biological, and linguistic phenomena. Clinical Psychology, by definition, is the study of the assessment, diagnosis, and treatment of mental illness or mental disorders. Clinical Psychology includes dealing with various mental conditions, including depression, manic depression bipolar disorder, and schizophrenia. Clinical Psychology integrates science, theory, and clinical knowledge about a total person. The gist of this book, the "Philosophy of Integration of Medical Anthropology and Clinical Psychology," is to explore and put into the right perspectives, the understanding of human (*Anthropos*), in Greek and the soul, (*Psych*), in Greek, originally, meaning "the soul, mind, spirit" or invisible entity that occupies the physical body. This book explores the integration of Medical Anthropology and Clinical Psychology, putting the right perspective of human biology and the soul.

I dedicate this book to my five children, Blessing Qhawelenkosi, Shalom Sinqobile, Prosper Thandolwenkosi, Emmanuel Nkosilathi, and Joseph Nkosana who love sciences, and my lovely wife, Judith Gasela Mhlanga, for encouragement, inspiration, and support. This book is also dedicated to Leeroy, Milile, Zion Nyathi, Nomasonto Nxumalo, Barbara Sibanda, Catherine and Jeremiah Pemberton, Marsha, Priscilla Mutisi, Munirah, Maka and Phetheni and Sibusiso Ndlovu. I also dedicate this book to the University of Washington where I did my non-matriculated Ph.D. and to Walden University in Minnesota where I did my Clinical Psychology-Forensic Ph.D. The courses I took from these two Universities, conscientious of my love for Medical Anthropology and Clinical Psychology, have shone a light on the quest for biology and soul, mind, and spirit. In Medical Anthropology, human health, diseases, treatment, and prevention will be discussed in depth. In Clinical Psychology, mental health issues for both the adolescents and adults will be explored and analyzed for the impact it has been on human health.

INTRODUCTION

This book has been written with a lot of thought, desire, and intellectual pursuit with the quest to understand the integration of Medical Anthropology and Clinical Psychology. Medical Anthropology is the study of human health, disease, treatment, prevention, and health care system. This includes the scientific study of humanity, human behavior, human biology, culture, linguistics, and societies, in the past, present, and future. Medical Anthropology investigates and examines people's health and illness in the context of understanding their bodies and souls. Medical Anthropology draws upon social, cultural, biological, and linguistic phenomena. Clinical Psychology, by definition, is the study of the assessment, diagnosis, and treatment of mental illness or mental disorders. Clinical Psychology includes dealing with various mental conditions, including depression, manic depression bipolar disorder, and schizophrenia. Clinical Psychology integrates science, theory, and clinical knowledge about a total person. The gist of this book, the "Philosophy of Integration of Medical Anthropology and Clinical Psychology," is to explore and put into the right perspectives, the understanding of human (*Anthropos*), in Greek and the soul, (*Psych*), in Greek, originally, meaning "the soul, mind, spirit" or invisible entity that occupies the physical body. This book explores the integration of the understating of Medical Anthropology and Clinical Psychology, putting to order human biology and the soul.

In this book, Medical Anthropology will be defined, discussed, and explored to understand its origins, its purpose, and what it anticipates achieving human in development in societies, linguistics, archaeology, cultures, and biology. In the same vein, Clinical Psychology will be discussed, explored, and analyzed for its impact on human health, including children's health and young adults and adults.

Chapter One discusses Medical Anthropology. Chapter Two explores Clinical Psychology. Chapter three elucidates Biblical health for the body, mental capability, soul, and spirit. Chapter Three contrasts the Medical versus Biblical approach toward human health. Furthermore, in Chapter Four, the contrast is explored between Psychology and Biblical solutions to human health. The branches of Medical Anthropology such as Biomedical, Sociomedical, and Epistemology are explored. Chapter Five of the book discusses Medical Anthropology and Archeology theory and methods, Empirical methods, and Biocultural that impact human health. Government and

Civil Society's impacts on human health are explored also. Medical Anthropology and Clinical Psychology are summarized, to conclude the chapters. This is my 8th book, and this book means a lot to me and it is more interesting and fascinating because it reveals my passion to reach out to human health and human soul. Buckle up, friends, and get ready to peruse and plunge into the oasis of knowledge and wisdom of God, displayed in humanity. You will learn about human ingenuity, human capabilities, human endeavors, human innovation, and of course, human limitations and uncertainties as they struggle and wrestle with self-identity, self-awareness, social awareness, and their destiny until they sought the sovereign creator and sustainer of the source of life, God.

CHAPTER ONE

Medical Anthropology

Medical Anthropology is the study of human health, disease, treatment, prevention, and health care systems. This includes the scientific study of humanity, human behavior, human biology, culture, linguistics, and societies, in the past, present, and future. Medical Anthropology investigates and examines people's health and illness in the context of understanding their bodies and souls. Medical Anthropology draws upon social, cultural, biological, and linguistic phenomena. Clinical Psychology, by definition, is the study of the assessment, diagnosis, and treatment of mental illness or mental disorders. Clinical Psychology includes dealing with various mental conditions, including depression, manic depression, bipolar disorder, and schizophrenia. Clinical Psychology integrates science, theory, and clinical knowledge about a total person. The gist of this book, the "Philosophy of Integrating of Medical Anthropology and Clinical Psychology," is to explore and put into the right perspectives, the understanding of human (Anthropos), in Greek and the soul, (Psych), in Greek, originally, meaning "the soul, mind, spirit" or invisible entity that occupies the physical body.

Anthropology is the study of the origin and development of human societies and cultures. "Anthropology is the study of the origin and development of human societies and cultures. Culture is the learned behavior of people, including their languages, belief systems, social structures, institutions, and material goods. Anthropologists study the characteristics of past and present human communities through a variety of techniques. In doing so, they investigate and describe how different peoples of our world lived throughout history."[1] The contemporary uses of anthropology include self-improvement, preservation for posterity, advocate, cultural broker, solving conflicts, governance, and prevention of ill effects of technology. "As anthropologists study societies and cultures, they must evaluate their interpretations to make sure they are not

---

[1] https://education.nationalgeographic.org/resource/history-branches-anthropology, (Accessed May 25, 2022).

biased. This bias is known as ethnocentrism, or the habit of viewing all groups as inferior to another, usually their own, cultural group."[2]

Medical anthropology is conceptualized as the human health, disease, medication and prevention. It is the study of how medicine is practiced in the practical sense to improve human quality life and the standard of caring. Medical anthropology's key sections are biomedicine, ethnomedicine and health disparities. Biomedicine is defined as "the healing practice in specific cultures." It is imperative to understand the dynamics of cultures and their belief systems in relation to sickness, medication, and prevention. The tapping of local and indigenous knowledge and material that is effective in diagnosis, treatment and care is fundamental in medical anthropology. Ethnomedicine is defined as the "healing practices followed by a specific or particular people identified as a culture." People in particular cultures have their own understanding about the healing processes and medical procedures. Therefore, ethnomedicine defines a particular culture with its own medical and care system. Each culture is unique and follows its methodologies to achieve curing and healing practices. The definition of these terms has not changed but they have been expounded over the years since the world has become a global village. As a result, ethnomedicine, biomedicine and health disparities have been elucidated extensively to add the meanings of the terms according to the context of the culture. In practical terms, there is no much differences between what I learned in the class and the reality of the definition of the terms.

"Medical anthropology seeks to understand experience of sufferers in order to illuminate the human dimension of illness and health dynamics." Good asserts, "Western curing is aimed exclusively at the mechanical body, while Zinacanteco procedures is directed at social relations and supernatural agents." It means healthcare disparities focuses on some members of the community who can and cannot access healthcare services and facilities. The socioeconomic will, in most cases, disadvantage those who are with disabilities and those who are poor. The health disparities can prevent opportunities for those who have diseases, injuries, violence or other illnesses if they are no reviews for unequal benefits because of social status. I found out that the belief systems I learned in the class are like my culture and in relation to social and supernatural agents.

"Sickness" is a feeling of not well. This is not limited to body not functioning normal, but it includes emotional, psychological, and mental imbalance. According to Hugh and Lock, "Sickness is a form of communication through which nature, social and culture speak…" According to Singer and Baer, "Disease and illness are the result of biological processes. It exists within a cultural framework. Disease is the disruption in the dynamic 'steady state' of the body. Disease is a maladaptive state of body." The causes of illnesses and diseases varies from place to place. The examples are those from Yanomamo who believe that "Illnesses are caused by ghosts

---

[2] Ibid.

or spirit possessions, the Azande who believe that illness is caused by possession and sorcery, while other cultures believe that illnesses or diseases are caused by environmental imbalance (humoral system)."

Depression is caused by anxiety and frustration of life. Depression is still regarded as a taboo in my society and culture. There is a stigma about the depression. If my family, community, and the church learn that I am suffering from depression caused by stress, they would see me as a negative person who does not relate well with other people, my family and the community. The sole cause of depression in my culture is viewed emanating from the one who suffers from it. It is never thought that depression may be caused by external forces. The stigma of depression usually is left untreated. The treatment is also very expensive as one would need a specialist, professional psychologist or/and counselor. The process takes longer time hence the expense. The prescriptions are also expensive not easily accessible.

The patterns detected in my own health seeking behavior was the fact that depression is caused by stress as one wrestles with emotional and psychological challenges of life. Depression is now regarded as a chronic disease as it leads to breakdown and death if it is not addressed clinically or through counseling. Many people who are suffering from depression do not seek help or medication because it is a taboo in my culture because of its stigma. Treatment of depression is also compounded by race disparities in which minorities do not have access to quality care because of their social status compared to those who have higher income per capita. The minorities receive less intensive care. Social economic status (SES) matters in different communities. "Poverty is a negative health status multiplier because poor living condition leads to disease risk and poorer nutrition leads to lower growth."

The experiential health which leads to feelings of tranquility and fulfilment is the goal for functional health. Biomedicine, ethnomedicine and health disparities bring curing and or healing within cultural systems of individuals according to their culture.

Anthropology has some branches that include cultural anthropology also called social anthropology, linguistic anthropology, biological and physical anthropology, and archaeology. "Biological anthropology, also known as physical anthropology, is the study of the evolution of human beings and their living and fossil relatives. Biological anthropology places human evolution within the context of human culture and behavior. This means biological anthropologists look at how physical developments, such as changes in our skeletal or genetic makeup, are interconnected with social and cultural behaviors throughout history."[3] Linguistic anthropology is the study of how language influences social life and people who live in certain areas. Linguistic anthropology provides people with language, the intellectual tools for thinking and acting in the world to resonate with their environment.

"Biological anthropology, also known as physical anthropology, is the study of the

---

[3] Ibid.

evolution of human beings and their living and fossil relatives. Biological anthropology places human evolution within the context of human culture and behavior. This means biological anthropologists look at how physical developments, such as changes in our skeletal or genetic makeup, are interconnected with social and cultural behaviors throughout history."[4] These trace back on how humans evolved earlier and the progressive development. Human skills in developing tools, the study of human skeletons and other parts of human remains, to understand human food, diet, behaviors is called human paleontology, or paleoanthropology in relation to their social and cultural practices. Archaeology is one other branch of anthropology that shades light to the human past. "Archaeology is the study of the human past using material remains. These remains can be any objects that people created, modified, or used. Archaeologists carefully uncover and examine these objects to interpret the experiences and activities of peoples and civilizations throughout history."[5] The relationships with other people and cultures. Anthropology basically reflects the evolving relationship between people and cultures.

The evolutionists have the school of thought that humans originated from apes. "Modern humans originated in Africa within the past 200,000 years and evolved from their most likely recent common ancestor, Homo erectus, which means 'upright man' in Latin. Homo erectus is an extinct species of human that lived between 1.9 million and 135,000 years ago."[6] As a matter of fact, the evolutionists assert that the human lineage has five stages evolved from the Apes: Australopithecus Afarensis, Homo Habilis, Homo Erectus, Homo Neanderthalensis and Homo Sapiens. This school of thought was popularized by Charles Dawne, who taught a theory of "The survival of the fittest." He argued that all living humans belong to one species and that its "races" all descended from a single ancestor. Thousands if not millions of stone tools, paintings, footprints, uncountable traces of human behavior in the prehistoric record indicate the origin of humans are from Africa, asserts Charles Dawne. This is a point of departure with Charles Dawne school of thought as the creation theory apologists vehemently, argue their case against Dawne. Their belief system declares that human beings were created in the image of God, (*Imago Dei*) and the creation theory has substantial evidence about human beings having been created by God, but I will not discuss it here in this book.

God created all things by his command; however, when God made man, as the crown of his handiwork, there was a dialogue within the Godhead. For God to create man at the end of all creation was an honor and favor. Before man was created, God completely filled the earth with vegetation and animals, a provision for man's survival. God created man with wisdom, unlike any created animals before him. The verse brings in the divine revelation of the Trinity. When God was creating, He said, "Let there be . . ." but when man was made, God made a

---

[4] Ibid.

[5] Ibid.

[6] https://www.google.com/search?q=humans+evolved+from+apes, (Accessed March 19, 2023).

consultation: "Let us make man in Our own *image*, according to Our *likeness*," (Genesis 1:26, NKJV). In creating the universe, vegetation and animals, God used authority and command, but it was with affection that he created man. The three persons of the Trinity consulted and concurred to make man.

Man was made in God's image and after his likeness. These two words express the same thing about *imago Dei*. When verse 26 is examined closer, the interpretation of plural pronouns "let us," "our image," and our "likeness" draw attention to the identity of the Creator. Mathews continues,

> Regarding the verb "make," we have already observed at 1:1 that the verbs "made" (*asa*) and "created" (*bara*) are in parallel both structurally and semantically in 2.4a, b. Here the parallel between v.26 ("Let us make") and v.27 ("So God created") indicates that they are virtual synonyms.[7]

The dialogue within the Godhead displays divine honor in creating human life. Gordon J. Wenham explains, "It refers to the 'fullness of attributes and powers conceived as united within the Godhead."[8] One would concur with the suggestion that it is the plural of fullness.

I will refer you to the Holy Bible for a precise answer about where human beings came from.

With that background of anthropology and the branches mentioned above, we now turn to Medical Anthropology.

What is Medical Anthropology

Medical anthropology is the subsection of anthropology that captures social, cultural, biological, and linguistics of human health and way of life. It focuses on human health, disease, treatment of sicknesses, healing process and prevention of diseases. Medical anthropology is also defined as follows, "Medical anthropology is the study of how human health and illness are shaped, experienced, and understood in light of global, historical, and political forces…the complexity of disease states, diagnostic categories, and what comes to count as pathology or health."[9] Medical anthropology taps from health culture as bioscientific epidemiology, and the social construction of knowledge and politics of science as scientific discovery and hypothesis testing. This includes micro and macro politics that narrates the governance of the social systems in the land or cultures.

---

[7] Kenneth A. Mathews, *Genesis 1-11:26*, The New American Commentary, vol. 1A Nashville: Broadman & Holman, 1996.

[8] Gordon J. Wenham, *Genesis 1-15*, Word Biblical Commentary, vol. 1 (Waco, TX: Word, 1987), 28.

[9] https://anthropology.stanford.edu/research-projects/medical-anthropology, (Accessed May 28, 2022).

Medical anthropology has been around since 1963 as an empirical research, social and cultural representation of health, illness, and care practices in the health sector as human intervention for better health. Medical anthropology has expanded to include international health across the globe. It includes the cycle of infection, nutrition interventions in promoting breastfeeding promotion, growth monitoring, weaning foods, nutrition education, diet that include vitamin A supplements, iron, iodine, artificial supplements in PHC and other micronutrients. Medical anthropology is also referred to as a philosophical study on health and illness. Scientific biomedicine and social medicine influence social and cultural variables in epidemiology and in pathology. Medical anthropology, furthermore, seeks to develop medical knowledge and medical care systems and the integration of the interaction of social, environmental and biological factors to influence health and illness in any given community or society. Medical anthropology takes into consideration the political economy of health provision and political ecology of infectious, borne, chronic diseases, and malnutrition to captivate the essence of health.

Medical Anthropology as a Discipline

Medical anthropology as a discipline is focused on studies on illness, treatment, healing, medical care, and biotechnologies. "These also include studies of contemporary modes of subjectivity and human experience; violence, suffering and humanitarian interventions; moral dimensions of medicine, illness, and global health; cultural studies of biomedicine and emerging biotechnologies; race, ethnicity, and health care disparities; anthropologies of infectious diseases and global health delivery; and anthropological studies of major mental illness, stigma, and mental health services."[10] It is a multifaceted discipline that touches all forms of human health, diseases, illnesses, treatment and prevention. Medical anthropology as a discipline, explores and integrates social, cultural, medical, and biological approaches. The understanding of human biological adaptation and evolutionary basis through the study of ecological, demographical, genetic, developmental paleontological, behavioral, and epidemiological; dimensions of human adaptation are the foundations of Medical Anthropology. Medical Anthropology as a discipline study how people in different cultural settings experience health and illnesses. In various backgrounds and different settings, Medical Anthropology relates to sickness, moral, religious, cultural, and community ethos.

---

[10] https://ghsm.hms.harvard.edu/research/medical-anthropology, (Accessed May 30, 2022).

The fundamentals of Medical Anthropology to Human Health

The medical anthropological approach has so much to offer for interventions for understanding human illnesses and behaviors. Some of the examples in the following capture the essence of medical anthropology in different countries, science, and psychiatry in the Middle East. Doostdar traces the rise of the "psych" sciences in Iran in the early 20th century. El Shakry traces the rise of Freudian (psycho) analysis in Egypt in the mid-20th century. Doostdar-Empiricism, Spiritism, in Iran, and attempts to contact the dead were grounded in science in many places. As in the "West", the borderland between "religion" and science was permeable. New sciences like psychology put the "non-empirical" out for public consideration. Even "Spiritism" was seen as an attempt to tame the chaos of falling onto rational lines. These efforts at systematization are part of broader efforts to root out corruption.

Spiritism and Experimentation were part of "ma-rafat al ruh" – the science of spirit/psyche. It parallels the efforts in Europe and Iran to explain inexplicable behaviors, hysteria, possession, and other mental phenomena. Behrouzan seeks to trace how "depreshen" talk became increasingly prevalent in Iran (1990). She traces this circulation of the term and the diagnoses, using interviews, surveys, diaries, and conversations. Depression and "Depreshen" medicalization are everyday experiences that are transformed into medical events, conditions, and processes, and mental illness is a common space of medicalization. Behrouz acknowledges the statistical picture of a rise in depression.

Reflecting upon an illness or injury episode in relation to "Biomedicine," "Ethnomedicine," and/or health disparities, it is imperative to understand the various patterns that emerge when people find themselves sick. It is common knowledge that when people get sick, they find alternative ways to determine and use various knowledge to find solutions. Biomedicine is defined as "the healing practice in specific cultures."[11] It is imperative to understand the dynamics of cultures and their belief systems in relation to sickness, medication and prevention. The tapping of local and indigenous knowledge and material that is effective in diagnosis, treatment and care is fundamental in medical anthropology. Ethnomedicine is defined as the "healing practices followed by a specific or particular people identified as a culture."[12]

People in particular cultures have their own understanding about the healing processes and medical procedures. Therefore, ethnomedicine defines a particular culture with its own medical and care system. Each culture is unique and follows its methodologies to achieve curing and healing practices. The definition of these terms has not changed but they have been expounded over the years due to the fact that the world has become a global village. As a result, ethnomedicine, biomedicine and health disparities have elucidated extensively to add the

---

[11] Seth, Messinger, *ANTH 215 A*, Lecture 3, 22, 2018, p. 21.
[12] Ibid. p. 17.

meanings of the terms according to the context of the culture. "Medical anthropology seeks to understand experience of sufferers in order to illuminate the human dimension of illness and health dynamics."[13] Good asserts, "Western curing is aimed exclusively at the mechanical body, while Zinacanteco procedures is directed at social relations and supernatural agents."[14]

It means healthcare disparities focuses on some members of the community who can and cannot access healthcare services and facilities. The socioeconomic will, in most cases, disadvantage those who are with disabilities and those who are poor. The health disparities can prevent opportunities for those who have diseases, injuries, violence or other illnesses if they are no reviews for unequal benefits because of social status. "Sickness" is a feeling of not well. This is not limited to body not functioning normal, but it includes emotional, psychological and mental imbalance. According to Hugh and Lock, "Sickness is a form of communication through which nature, social and culture speak…"[15] According to Singer and Baer, "Disease and illness are the result of biological processes. It exists within a cultural framework. Disease is the disruption in the dynamic 'steady state' of the body. Disease is a maladaptive state of body."[16] The causes of illnesses and diseases varies from place to place. The examples are those from Yanomamo who believe that "Illnesses are caused by ghosts or spirit possessions, the Azande who believe that illness is caused by possession and sorcery, while other cultures believe that illnesses or diseases are caused by environmental imbalance (humoral system)."[17]

Medical Anthropology on Human Diseases

Depression is caused by anxiety and frustration of life. Depression is still regarded as a taboo in my society and culture. There is a stigma about the depression. If my family, community and the church learn that I am suffering from depression caused by stress, they would see me as a negative person who does not relate well with other people, my family and the community. The sole cause of depression in my culture is viewed emanating from the one who suffers from it. It is never thought that depression may be caused by external forces. The stigma of depression usually is left untreated. The treatment is also very expensive as one would need a specialist, professional psychologist or/and counselor. The process takes longer time hence the expense. The prescriptions are also expensive not easily accessible.

The patterns detected in my own health seeking behavior was the fact that depression is caused by stress as one wrestles with emotional and psychological challenges of life. Depression

---

[13] Ibid. p. 9.

[14] Bryan J. Good, *Medicine, Rationality and Experience*, (New York: University of Cambridge Press, 1994), 27.

[15] Scheper, Hugh, and Lock, *ANTH 215 A*, Lecture 1, 2018, p.33.

[16] Messinger, *ANTH 215 A*, Lecture 3, January 22 and 24, 2018, p. 2,3,4.

[17] Messinger, Lecture 3, 22, 224, 2018, p. 8

is now regarded as a chronic disease as it leads to breakdown and death if it is not addressed clinically or through counseling. Many people who are suffering from depression do not seek help or medication because it is a taboo in my culture because of its stigma. Treatment of depression is also compounded by race disparities in which minorities do not have access to quality care because of their social status compared to those who have higher income per capita. The minorities receive less intensive care. Social-economic status (SES) matters in different communities. "Poverty is a negative health status multiplier because poor living condition leads to disease risk and poorer nutrition leads to lower growth."[18]

Experiential health which leads to feelings of tranquility and fulfilment is the ultimate goal for functional health. Biomedicine, ethnomedicine and health disparities bring curing and or healing within cultural systems of individuals according to their culture. Some of the concepts presented in the class are congruent with my belief system. I believe that health care should be grounded in scientific rationales although community-shared experiences should be given space to explore local and indigenous knowledge for healthcare systems. I see the body as a coherent whole but made up of different parts as a puzzle that fit together to make one beautiful community.

Medical Anthropology on Human Treatment

Ethics is the social system adopted by a society or a culture. Ethics depicts the standards or the codes of the behavior of a family, a society or a group of people. Ethics entails choices and actions agreed upon by a group of people groups or individuals as norms that would guide a particular people.

According to Mattingly in her 'moral laboratory' asserts, "The day-to-day experimental living space where moral/ethical are made...Experience is part of time and future decisions and actions are grounded in history."[19] Kleinman propounds, in congruent with Mattingly, "Seen in this light, moral processes differ in fundamental way from ethical course. The latter is an abstract articulation and debate over codified value."[20] Experience is a moral process based on a societal and ethical codes which are acceptable in a culture. "Mattingly uses 'moral' and 'ethical' exchangeable, drawing a distinction between ethical and moral, universal and moral local."[21] He uses both ethics and morals to assert that all are "working to achieve a

---

[18] Messinger, *ANTH 215 A*, Lecture 4, January 29, 31, 2018, p. 9.

[19] Cheryl Mattingly, Moral laboratories: Family Peril and the Struggle for Good Life, (Berkeley, CA: University of California, Press, 2014), 35.

[20] Arthur Kleinman, *Experience and its Moral Modes: Culture and Human Conditions and Disorder*, The Tanner Lectures on Human Value, (Stanford University: April 13-16, 1998), 363.

[21] Seth Messinger, Lecture 4, January 29, 2018, p. 29.

socially recognized 'good life' and it is widely shared across cultures (universal)."[22] Kleinman discusses ethics and moral, "Ethical discourse is usually principle-based, with meta-theoretical commentary on the authorization and implication of those principles. (in bioethics, the chief principles are autonomy, beneficence, and justice; they in turn privilege informed consent and confidentiality). Ethical discourse is reflective and intellectualist, emphasizing cognition (more precisely, in today's jargon, and rationale choice), over affect or behavior and coherence over the sense of incompleteness and unknowability and uncontrollability that is so prevalent in ordinary life."[23] Drawing from both Mattingly and Kleinman's concepts and the definition of ethics, one would define ethics as social rules/codes adopted by a society to live by. Morals are personal characters of individuals within the society. Therefore, ethics are socially acceptable codes or rules of behavior in a society. These sets of rules or principles in the society are to curb misconducts and crimes in a society.

In the state of Kentucky where I lived for the past six years, marijuana is an illegal drug. Mattingly's "moral laboratories" resonate with many families who view the drug as part of social goods for the societies and families into making hard decisions for the loved ones to treat the disease hence phenomenologically, ethics and moral practice collide in that context.

Children who suffer from seizures, and medically, it has been proven that marijuana can cure patients suffering from seizures but it is still an ethical and moral issue in some of the states in USA to legalize it as treatment for certain diseases and illnesses. This could be the only treatment the drug can offer to treat a patient. The possibilities of trying to achieve a good life for a family member who is sick and to have the only drug for the treatment available could be a game changer for families to opt to use marijuana for the treatment of their family member. But this demands the ethical and moral decisions for the family to do it.

It is very imperative to understand that some situation in life can force people to make choices contrary to their conscience, faith, moral, ethics and belief system in order to correct something wrong in someone's life or family. Such a background can impact one's ethical practices in ordinary life as one pursues the path to helping someone while putting aside the interests of self or family. It is indeed, counting the cost in order to empathize with the victim, suffering from an illness or social injustice, racism, crime or purely giving up moral and ethical rights on behalf someone else to make a difference in the society.

---

[22] Messinger, Lecture 4, 33.
[23] Kleinman, 363.

Medical Anthropology on Prevention of Diseases: Ebola, Sars, Malaria, COVID-19, HIV/AIDS.

The two fundamental prevention and control of diseases are categorized as first in identifying and understanding the nature of the disease such as its mutation, the cause and the treatment that has been discovered. The second is applying relevant health interventions that are incorporated into education and health systems to curb and prevent the diseases in question. "Anthropology's role conventionally has been in the translation of local concepts of illness and treatment, and the adaptation of biomedical knowledge to fit local aetiologias. Medical anthropology plays an important role in examining the local context of disease diagnosis, treatment and prevention, and the structural as well as conceptual barriers to improved health status,"[24] With infectious diseases witnessed globally, such as Ebola, Sars, Malaria, HIV/AIDS, Covid-19, and other diseases, it is important for health services to be aware of the impact and draw some measures to treat and prevent the spread.

EBOLA

Ebola is believed by the researchers that it originated from animals such as monkeys, chimpanzees or fruit bats. It is a virus with various strains that causes Ebola hemorrhagic fever in humans. The symptoms of the disease start like flu and it progress rapidly to internal bleeding, organ damage. The virus is transmitted through bodily fluids. The symptoms include fever, sore throat, headaches, diarrhea, bleeding, muscular pain. The medication applied is Antoltivimab/maftivmab/odesivimab (Inmazeb).

SARS

Severe Acute Respiratory Syndrome (SARS) is a viral respiratory disease caused by SARS which appeared in China in 2002 which spread globally. It is a contagious disease that is fatal respiratory illness caused by coronavirus. It is transmitted through droplets that enter the air through coughing, sneezing, talks, breathing from an infected person. The symptoms are dry cough, fever, headaches, muscle aches, difficult, in breathing. "SARS is an airborne virus and can spread through small droplets of saliva in a similar way to the cold and influenza. It was the first severe and readily transmissible new disease to emerge in the 21st century and showed

---

[24] National Library of Medicine: *National Center for Biotechnology, Article,* https://pubmed.ncbi.nlm.nih.gov/9892288/, 2018, (Accessed August 30, 2022).

a clear capacity to spread along the routes of international air travel. SARS can also be spread indirectly via surfaces that have been touched by someone who is infected with the virus."[25] SARS is one of the infectious diseases that rocked the world emanating from Asia. However, it was quickly contained from 2002 to 2004 between the ages of 25 to 70 years old although some few cases of children under 15 years old appeared here and there.

There is no cure, treatment or vaccines for SARS but controlling the outbreaks and containing the disease through early detection of cases and isolation, identifying sources of infection, quarantine suspected individuals for ten days, and personal prevention measures are key to curb the spread.

Malaria

Malaria is caused by a single-celled parasite of the genus plasmodium. The parasite is transmitted to humans by mosquito bites, a female anopheles. "They are 430 Anopheles mosquito species known around the world, roughly 30 or 4 are vectors (transmitters). The symptoms include fever, chills, headaches, muscle aches, fatigue, nausea, vomiting and diarrhea. The infection can cause kidney failure, seizure, disorientation, coma, and possibly death."[26] Malaria is transmitted by infected mosquitos, especially, from hot and humid places like Africa and also in South America, Eastern Europe, South and Eastern Asia and in Islands in the Central and South and Pacific Oceans. Malaria is not caused by a virus like other infectious diseases or by a bacterium but it is caused by the parasites.

Prevention and Treatment of Malaria

When one is infected by Malaria, it is important to get treatment as soon as possible to kill the parasites. Malaria drugs that are effect include, artemisinin drugs, chloroquine, quinine, atovaquone, Mefloquine and other specific drugs for malaria. These drugs have proven that they can cure malaria. Those who are planning to travel to visit these areas mentioned above, should take preventative medication that may reduce the risks of contracting malaria. One should be aware and avoid being bitten by mosquitoes. To lower the risks of getting malaria, these are some of the precautions, "Apply mosquito repellent DEET (diethyltoluamide), Drape mosquito netting over beds, Put screens on windows and doors. Treat clothing, mosquito nets, tents, sleeping bags and other fabrics with an insect repellent called permethrin, and wear long

---

[25] https://www.who.int/health-topics/severe-acute-respiratory-syndrome#tab=tab_1,.
[26] https://www.orkin.com, (Accessed August 30, 2022).

pants and long sleeves to cover your skin,"[27] These drugs were developed and tested in Kenya, Ghana and Malawi as a pilot program to lead on treatment and prevention medication.

HIV/AIDS

The HIV/AIDS holds a lot of myths and hypothesis about its origin. It is imperative to understand how and when AIDS came into existence to have adequate information and to know how to deal with this complex disease. According to Sam Puckett and Alan Emery,

> the AIDS virus made its first appearance during the 1960s or earlier in several countries in South Central Africa. The virus is one of a particular class of viruses known as retrovirus. . . . This new form of retrovirus has been named by its various discoveries as "Human T-Lymphotropic Virus Type III" (HTLV-3), "Lymphadenopathy Associated Virus" (LAV) and AIDS Retro Virus (ARV). In 1986 an international science committee gave it the official designation "Human Immuno-deficiency Virus," or "HIV." To the public it is known as "the AIDS virus" and the medical condition it causes is known as "AIDS"—Acquired Immune Deficiency Syndrome.[28]

The AIDS virus is one of the scariest and most feared diseases in human history. HIV/AIDS is an infectious disease caused by the Human Immunodeficiency Virus (HIV).
Betty Moffatt explains,

> Acquired Immune Deficiency syndrome (AIDS) is the result of a defect in the immune system's family ability to resist certain types of infections: those caused by viruses, fungi, parasites, and mycobacteria (tuberculosis-like organism). . . . It means that AIDS is not a disease in itself. The mortality rate from AIDS comes from the body's inability to resist what is known as 'opportunistic infections.[29]

According to Moffatt, the person dies from the failure of the body's immune system to defend against illnesses:

---

[27] https://my.clevelandclinic.org/health/diseases/15014-malaria, (Accessed September 5, 2022).
[28] Sam B. Puckett and Alan R. Emery, *Managing AIDS in the Workplace* (Reading, MA: Addison, 1988), 1.
[29] Betty Clare Moffat, *When Someone You Know Has AIDS: A Book of Hope for Family and Friends* (Santa Monica, CA: IBS, 1986), 34.

Living with AIDS description of the medical diagnosis of AIDS as affecting the immune system in ways currently under study and revision by researchers. . . . The term "acquired" is used because people with AIDS are known to have normal immune system function prior to the onset of the syndrome.[30]

Some misconceptions about HIV/AIDS infections make it more feared. Since its discovery, the origin of HIV/AIDS has been a mystery. Although there have been many theories of its origin, these hypotheses cannot be substantiated in record. Scientists do not know how the AIDS virus came into existence and where it first appeared in human history. In trying to determine the origins of HIV/AIDS, Lyn Frumkin and John Leonard assert,

An AIDS-like virus causing Simian Acquired Immunodeficiency Syndrome in monkeys has been isolated. A different retrovirus related to HIV has been isolated recently from wild Africa have found cases of unexplained opportunistic infections in patients as early as 1975, that today would meet the current CDC definition of AIDS. It seems likely that the current epidemic may have first occurred somewhere in Central Africa in the mid-1970s.[31]

The speculation of the origins is likely to go on for years.

The hypothesis cannot be proven; however, some scientists speculate that AIDS first appeared in America among homosexuals. Frumkin and Leonard write,

In mid-1981, usual opportunistic infections began to occur in homosexuals and users of intravenous drugs in United States. The infections proved to be uniformly fatal and unprecedented in severity in these previously healthy individuals. This apparently new condition was named the acquired immunodeficiency syndrome, or AIDS.[32]

The claim about its origin cannot be proven. Its origin, mutation, nature, and weaknesses continue to baffle scientists, though hypotheses about origin and nature have shed some glimpses of light.

The transmission most of the HIV/AIDS infection occurs through sexual intercourse with infected persons. Promiscuous heterosexuals lead the highest infections of HIV/AIDS. HIV/

---

[30] Ibid., 35.
[31] Lyn Robert Frumkin and John Martin Leonard, *Questions & Answers on AIDS* (Oradell, NJ: Medical Economics, 1987), 12.
[32] Ibid., 1.

AIDS transmission also occurs through using needles previously used by an infected person. HIV/AIDS can be transmitted if unsterilized needles are shared.

In some cases, transmission can take place through pregnancy, child-mother transmissions, or through breastfeeding. If a mother is infected with HIV/AIDS, she will likely give birth to an infected baby.

Blood transfusions are another way in which HIV/AIDS may be contracted. If a pregnant woman loses too much blood during delivery, if a person needs blood after being involved in an accident, or even during surgery, when unscreened donated blood is used in transfusion, infections can occur. However, the risk of getting HIV/AIDS infection through blood products has dramatically reduced in recent years.

Medical Consequences of HIV/AIDS

The medical consequences of HIV/AIDS are immense. Decades of research has attempted to find a prevention and cure for HIV/AIDS. Almond asserts,

> HIV consists of two main elements, an outer membrane or envelope, and an inner core. The outer membrane is taken from the cells of the person it infects. As a result, the virus survives extremely poorly outside the body. The infection caused by the virus is a productive infection, in which new virus particles are being produced for all or most of the duration of infection. This means the person is infectious for life.[33]

The HIV/AIDS positive person becomes infectious in weeks after becoming infected and before the immune's response develops into AIDS.

When the virus destroys the infected person's immune system, the person is prone to various other diseases. Shepherd and Smith propound,

> The virus is matter which border by definition between living and nonliving material. They are actually replicable protein matter which exists in a parasitic sense and can survive only as long as their hosts exist. HIV belongs to a class known as retroviruses because its reproduction process involves the virus using its reverse transcriptase enzyme to replicate its RNA into DNA molecules.[34]

---

[33] Almond, *AIDS*, 27.

[34] Shepherd Smith and Anita Moreland Smith, "Christians in the Age of AIDS," accessed May 2, 2012, http://www.allbookstores.com/Christians-Age-AIDS-Shepherd-Smith.

The HIV virus is complex, and its medical consequences have great impact both in the medical field and to the infected persons.

The available HIV/AIDS drugs (antiviral drugs) do not effectively kill the HIV virus; instead, they slow the progression of the disease in the body. Smith explains,

> The white blood cells that the virus attacks are T4 lymphocytes, monocytes, and macrophages. The invading virus turns the monocytes and macrophages into virus-producing factories for the rest of the individual's life but does not significantly damage the cell. Meanwhile, the T4 lymphocytes are systematically killed off over time.[35]

When the virus destroys the infected person's immune system, the person is prone to various other diseases. AIDS is a complex disease in which the virus unpredictably mutates so that it is difficult to find a medication that could destroy and eliminate its incubation in the body. Almond purports,

> The key biological property of HIV is its specific attack on certain cells of the body, the T 'helper' cells and macrophages of the immune system; this leads to its capacity to cause disease. . . . Thus, individual risk is a function not only of what subpopulation they belong to but which one their partners is from, or has had contact with, and so on.[36]

Almond continues,

> HIV antibody testing has therefore been used as a surrogate for the infection itself, since anyone who develops antibodies must have acquired persistent infection, given the nature of HIV. Following infection people are initially asymptomatic for several years and may remain so indefinitely; some have enlarged lymph nodes. HIV causes progressive damage to immune system or nervous system, leading to symptomatic disease.[37]

HIV develops into AIDS, which leads to severe damage to cell-mediated immunity that exposes the patient to opportunistic infections. As the patient would be susceptible to minor opportunistic infections and his/her immunity is compromised because of the HIV infection,

---

[35] Ibid.

[36] Almond, *AIDS—A Moral Issue*, 27.

[37] Ibid., 31.

he/she cannot resist any disease that can attack—so even a disease that is normally not fatal can easily cause death.

Prevention of HIV/AIDS.

HIV/AIDS prevention demands teamwork as well as individual responsibility to prevent the spread of the disease. As such, strategies have been discovered that can help to combat HIV/AIDS infections and prevent the spread of the disease. Epidemic infection of HIV/AIDS is caused by several reasons. Land gives suggests,

> These young people, lacking other means of support, may engage in sex in exchange for food, money, drugs, or shelter. In addition, children who have histories of sexual and physical abuse may lack the self-esteem to insist on safer sex even when they are aware of the risks. . . . Many homeless women who test positive for HIV trade sex for money and drugs.[38]

Regardless of the challenges that are mentioned above, preventive methods must be initiated to curb the spread of the disease.

HIV/AIDS prevention education is critical and necessary to buffer the spread of the disease. HIV/AIDS prevention education must be provided through literature, television, radio, and all social media. Prevention education must also be provided through seminars, conferences in churches, schools, prisons, the community and in companies and organizations. Outreach efforts in the streets, communities, and homeless shelters are fundamental in prevention campaigns because public announcements on television and radio cannot be heard or seen by homeless people or those who do not have access to the media. Behavioral changes of sexual habits, such as prostitution, unprotected sex, adultery, fornication, and homosexuality, as well as reducing drug abuse, have been found to decrease HIV/AIDS infections.

For those already infected, an ideal drug to combat AIDS must be used. Scientists have discovered anti-viral drugs that boost the immune system. The HIV Treatment Information Base reposts,

> CD4 cells are a type of lymphocytes (white blood cell). They are an important part of the immune system. CD4 cells are sometimes called T-Cells. The normal

---

[38] Helen Land, *AIDS: A Complete Guide to Psychosocial Intervention* (Milwaukee: Family Service America, 1992), 188.

ranges for CD4 and CD8 counts varies depending on the lab and test, but for an HIV negative person a normal CD4 count is in the range 460 to 1600.[39]

Jager points out,

> Retrovirus, of which HIV is one, is situated as to build their genetic information into the gene bank of cell. When there is a failure to kill the virus or eliminate it from the body, replication of the virus should be arrested by a drug (virus stasis) or it should be prevented from attacking cells.[40]

This is essential information for patients to take heed and apply. When medication has failed to cure AIDS, prevention must be emphasized in order to prevent the severe complications of opportunistic infections.

Adequate information on infections is critical for HIV/AIDS prevention. The use of sterile disposable needles prevents infection and use of condoms has been found effective if used. As a model to combat the spread of HIV/AIDS, pre and post-counseling is one of the means to help those with the disease. In pre-counseling, the counselor sits down with the counselee who is seeking to know his/her HIV/AIDS status before testing. In post-counseling, the counselee has completed the testing and is ready to receive the results. Post-counseling has some challenges, especially if the counselee is HIV/AIDS positive. If he/she is HIV/AIDS positive, the person is advised what to eat and how to live a healthy life, where, when, and how the antiviral drugs can be taken, and how they can help to boost immunity. If the test results are negative, the individual is given information and advised to prevent him/herself from contracting the disease.

Inoculation is another form of HIV/AIDS prevention. Jager asserts,

> Even in viral epidemics, this measure has proved an ideal weapon against a virus disease. Smallpox and infantile paralysis were eradicated by this means. . . .. HIV displays some peculiarities which render the development of a vaccine extraordinarily difficult. The external protein coating of HIV defeats established transformations by spontaneous mutation. This can be a historically important development in the virus's mechanism, so as to elude the antibodies directed against it by the immune system by changing the surface structures.[41]

Prevention is better than the cure. Prevention of the spread of HIV/AIDS is vital and needs to be spearheaded by church leaders.

---

[39] HIV Treatment Information Base, September 19, 2014, accessed October 5, 2016, www.*i-base.info.*

[40] Jager, *AIDS*, 40.

[41] Jager, *AIDS*, 38.

Additionally, breastfeeding can be avoided to prevent mother-to-child transmission of HIV/AIDS. Antiviral drugs have also been developed to prevent the transmission of HIV/AIDS while the child in still in the womb. The drug helps to prevent numerous infections of babies with HIV/AIDS. The next section discusses the treatment of HIV/AIDS.

Treatment of HIV/AIDS

Currently no treatment is available to destroy HIV/AIDS or restore the immune system. Richardson contends, "Research on antiviral drugs is being carried out in the United States and other countries in an attempt to provide a cure. Antiviral drugs are substances which interfere with the growth of reproduction viruses."[42] The challenge with antiviral drugs is that they often do not discriminate between infected cells and healthy cells Richardson continues,

> Another problem is that HIV is capable of infecting cells in the brain and other parts of the central nervous system. If an antiviral drug is not capable of passing through into the cerebrospinal fluid or the brain, and most are not, these infected cells may continue to produce more viruses.[43]

Antiviral drugs will continue to be a challenge because they cannot get rid of the HIV virus or they cannot utterly destroy all the infected cells.

The other drug that has been tested to put the infection into remission is Ribavarin. This drug can slow down the multiplication of HIV in the body. Richardson writes, "Further research is under way to assess its possible usefulness in the treatment of AIDS. Tests on the other antiviral agents, such as Suramin, HPA-23, and Ansamycin, have also demonstrated a reduction in the amount of virus present."[44] Antivirus drugs can significantly help to reduce or slow down the multiplication of the virus in the body of the infected person, but none of the drugs tested can cure AIDS.

HIV/AIDS educational programs can be part of the prevention of the disease. Siegel points out,

> Educational programs for staff, patients and families can provide accurate information to deal with real and imagined anxieties. . . . More importantly,

---

[42] Richardson, *Women and AIDS*, 23.

[43] Ibid.

[44] Ibid.

safer sex practice and no needle sharing should be practiced by everyone to prevent a whole variety of diseases, of which AIDS is the most serious.[45]

HIV/AIDS educational programs must be used to buffer further infections of the disease. The use of the antiviral drugs, which can influence the immune system, are continually tested. Richardson continues,

> Some of these immune-boosting drugs, such as Interfero. Others, like Cyclosporin, acts by suppressing the immune system. This latter approach to treatment stems from the theory that HIV works by tricking the immune system by destroying itself. . . . Made by Burroughs Wellcome, AZT has been tested mainly on AIDS patients who have pneumocystis. ATZ is not a cure for AIDS. Although it stops the virus from multiplying, it does not destroy it.[46]

Although there is no cure for AIDS, opportunistic infections can be treated. Moffatt asserts,

> There can be some improvements in AIDS conditions when the sound principles of nutrition, exercise, and following medical recommendations of the attending physician. Some AIDS persons have used the following to help fortify their immune systems and to create a more favorable climate for detoxification of existing viruses. Immuneplex, large doses of Vitamin C, Spirulina and LaPacho tea.[47]

Healthy eating and exercise do not cure but can help to boost the patient's immune system. Good diet helps HIV/AIDS patients live healthy lives even though they are infected. Moffatt writes, "Until a cure is found for AIDS and all its opportunistic manifestations, anything and everything that can increase the well-being of the AIDS person and help each one to rebuild his body defenses can be utilized with opportunistic results."[48] The following sections discuss the mythical beliefs about HIV/AIDS.

---

[45] Larry Siegel, *AIDS, and Substance Abuse* (New York: Haworth, 1987), 15.

[46] Richardson, *Women and AIDS*, 24.

[47] Moffatt, *When Someone You Love Has AIDS*, 131.

[48] Ibid., 132.Co

CORONAVIRUS/COVID-19

According to research, "SARS-CoV and MERS-CoV originated from bats. The SARS-CoV spread from infected civits to people. MERS-CoV spreads from infected dromedary camels' people. It is imperative to understand that the origin of SARS-CoV-2 which caused COVID-19 pandemic has not been proven."[49] Covid-19 is an infectious disease caused by the SARS-CoV-2 virus. Coronaviruses are a family of virus that is infectious. The infected person suffers from bronchos, failing to breath properly. The symptoms of the infection can start to show after 2-14 days after exposure of the virus. People who are at high risks are those with underlying medical conditions such as lung or heart diseases, diabetes, and other chronic diseases. The following are some of the symptoms patients infected by Covid-19: Fever or chills, Cough, Shortness of breath or difficulty breathing, Fatigue, Muscle or body aches, Headache, New loss of taste or smell, Sore throat, Congestion or runny nose, Nausea or vomiting and Diarrhea.

Most people infected with the virus will experience mild to moderate respiratory illness and recover without requiring special treatment…. Older people and those with underlying medical conditions like cardiovascular disease, diabetes, chronic respiratory disease, or cancer are more likely to develop serious illness. The best way to prevent and slow down transmission is to be well informed about the disease and how the virus spreads. Protect yourself and others from infection by staying at least 1 meter apart from others, wearing a properly fitted mask, and washing your hands or using an alcohol-based rub frequently. Get vaccinated when it's your turn and follow local guidance…. The virus can spread from an infected person's mouth or nose in small liquid particles when they cough, sneeze, speak, sing or breathe. These particles range from larger respiratory droplets to smaller aerosols. It is important to practice respiratory etiquette, for example by coughing into a flexed elbow, and to stay home and self-isolate until you recover if you feel unwell.

The Coronavirus or Covid-19, has caused a pandemic and respiratory illness that has affected the entire glob.

Conclusion

To recapture the fundamentals and the thrust of Medical Anthropology to conclude this chapter, it is imperative to understand the essence of Medical Anthropology as a discipline, the importance of Medical Anthropology to human health, human diseases, human treatment, and human prevention.

---

[49] https://www.google.com/search?q=coronavirus+origin, (Accessed August 31, 2022).

CHAPTER TWO

Clinical Psychology

Clinical Psychology, by definition, and according to Psychological Medicine, "Clinical psychology is an integration of social science, theory, and clinical knowledge for the purpose of understanding, preventing, and relieving psychologically based distress or dysfunction and to promote subjective well-being and personal development."[50] The central or the gist of its practice, it's about psychological assessment, clinical formulation, and psychotherapy. It is imperative to understand that clinical psychology also engages in research, teaching, consultation, forensic testimony, and focusing on development and administration to meet dire situations of patients who need the most pressing and deserving medical, emotional, and psychological needs.

How did Clinical Psychology begin? "The field is considered to have begun in 1896 with the opening of the first psychological clinical at the University of Pennsylvania by Lightner Witmer. In the first half of the 20th century, clinical psychology was focused on psychological assessment, with little attention given to treatment. This changed after the 1940s when World War II resulted in the need for a large increase in the number of trained clinicians."[51] Since then, three main educational models have been developed, the PhD Clinical Model, which is focused research purpose. The PhD Science-Practitioner Model, which basically, integrates the scientific research and practice models. The PsyD Science Practitioner-Scholar Model, focusing on clinical theory and practice. Clinical Psychology is quite different from psychiatry. The differences will be explored in the next chapters of this book. Stay tuned! The Clinical Psychology deals with various challenges patients or clients face.

---

[50] https://en.wikipedia.org/wiki/Clinical_psychology, (Accessed September 28, 2022).
[51] Ibid.

Case Study - Substance Use and the Adolescent

The cases of substance abuse related to disorders and its prevalence in the society. In mental health circles, the research shows that substance disorders are in the increase, especially with the adolescents. The risks and resilience factors and importance of accurate diagnosis is fundamental. An analysis of the case studies reviewed to consider specific characteristics of diagnosis on the bases of the DSM and appropriate treatment plans are valuable.

Substance abuse related disorder has wracked havoc in the society especially with the adolescents who have become addicted to certain drugs and alcohol abuse. Adolescents are in the developmental stage and have a great deal of independence to explore in life. Their independence has made them to explore even substance abuse has become an epidemic in US because of the freedom the adolescents have. Some of the theories regarding theories of the problems with substance include psychoanalytic, behavioral/cognitive behavioral and family systems. One example of common theories about the development and substance abuse is cognitive behavioral, (Burrow-Sanchez, J. J., 2006. P. 284. Para. 4.). This theory combines cognitive theory with social learning. "Cognitive behavioral theorists believe that substance abuse originates in an interaction between the person and his or her environment. Regarding adolescents, when they are faced with stressful situations (e.g., argument with a parent), they may manage these situations by using relevant coping skills," (Burrow-Sanchez, J. J. 2006. p. 284. Para. 4.).

The two main influential contextual risk factors that exist and allowing adolescents to indulge in substance abuse are drug laws and the availability of the substance. In the case of the client in the case study, the DSM diagnosis of the client is first to look at resilience conceptualization which is both social and health sciences that pose risks that are related to stress, depression, and health disorder. Despite questions raised about its cross-cultural equivalence, DSM is used widely across the world, for research purposes by investigators who seek to bring understanding and DSM, (Escobar, J. I., & Vega, W. A. 2006. p. 40. para. 2.)

People with personality disorder suffer isolation and loneliness because of the personal limitations that they have.

The rationale for assigning the client with anxiety disorder and schizophrenia. He is developing a personality disorder, showing in his behavior pattern, which is not consistent. He is consumed by himself, and he mentions that he does not need any friends at all.

Bipolar

Biblical Perspective: One of the main issues with modern psychology is that attempting to categorize everything into a diagnosis classifies even normal sadness and grief as a disorder. God designed sadness for a purpose. It is a biological and spiritual design that we need. Sadness helps us to look elsewhere for help. It brings the community of Christ together around the pain of others. In (2 Corinthians 7:8-11,NKJV), sorrow or sadness serves a useful purpose because it leads to repentance and salvation. (Good Mood, Bad Mood: Charles Hodges)

Intense and sometimes rapid fluctuations between self-exaltation and self-loathing are both distorted views a person holds alternately about themselves. Helping them to see the lies and what the truth God declares about them in Christ is the way forward. Bipolar is a disorder associated with episodes of mood swings of depression from low to manic high. Although the cause of bipolar is unknown but the environment and altered brain structure and chemistry can have great impact on an individual's behavior. The symptoms of bipolar are high or low energy, no motivation, no interest in daily activities, or insomnia. Jay Adam asserts, "In the downward cycling the depression certainly contributes to further failures as it often becomes the excuse for a faulty handling of sin itself. But, in contrast to those who would speak of changing the feelings in order to change the behavior, God reverses the order..."[52] The word of God is sufficient to counsel someone with bipolar disorder.

The Lord has ways to counsel people with bipolar disorders. Although this passage is not directly directed to bipolar disorder, king Saul of Israel had a spirit that bothered him all the time and God had a solution to soothe him through David. "Whenever the evil spirit from God bothered Saul, David would play his harp. Soul would relax and feel better..." (I Samuel 16:14-23, NKJV). For those who have insomnia, the Palmist concludes, "In vain you rise early and stay up late, toiling for food to eat-for he grants sleep to those he loves," (Psalm 127:2b, NKJV). This is not a direct rebuke to people, but this shows that God is concerned about one to sleep well and that He grants to those he loves. Some of the verses about those who are depressed, and God delivers them: (The righteous cry out, and the Lord hears them; he delivers them from all their troubles. The Lord is close to the broken-hearted and saves those who are crushed in spirit. The righteous person may have many troubles, but the Lord delivers him from them all," (Psalm 34:17-19, NKJV); "Why, my soul, are you downcast? Why so disturbed within me? Put your hope in God, for I will yet praise him, my Savior, and my God," (Psalm 42:11, NKJV); "But those who hope in the Lord will renew their strength. They will soar on wings like eagles; they will run and not weary, they will walk and not faint" (Isaiah 40;31, NKJV).

Codependent

A codependent is anyone who cannot function independently on his own. His/her thinking and behavior are organized around someone or substance. He/she puts more priority on others

---

[52] Jay E. Adam, The Christian Counselor's Manual, (Westminster: Presbyterian and Reformed Publishers), 1973, p. 377.

than himself/herself. He/she is a people pleaser and can plan his/her activity around pleasing an individual and trying to meet the needs of someone. Codependent is defined as, "Codependency refers to a mental, emotional, physical, and/or spiritual reliance on a partner, friend, or family member...Codependency is not a clinical diagnosis or a formally categorized personal disorder on its own. Generally speaking, codependency incorporates aspects of attachment style patterns developed in early childhood, and it can also overlap with other personality disorders, including dependent personality disorder."[53] (https://docs.google.com/document/d/1ORRkug4KmbcJq 6wsiMkuZoe2wJGLNy4ESvnVjjfXsJc/edit, Accessed February 2, 2021). This kind of person depends and relies on someone for his/her welfare. As stipulated, it is not a clinical diagnosis, but an individual can attach to someone although it can be associated with a disorder. It is due to a poor concept of self and poor boundaries that one fails to limit.

The Bible is very clear in that kind of pattern that one must depend and rely on God alone, not on an individual or substance. To be egocentric is a sin and it is humanistic. If one worships self, anyone, or anything it is idolatry. One can have a friend, a family member, or a partner but to depend and rely on them for one's survival is not approved in the Scripture except if someone has a special need. 'Even while we were still with you there with you, we gave you this rule: "He who does not work shall not eat," (II Thess. 3:10, NKJV). Some of the Bible verses that discourage dependence on others "So that you may walk properly before outsiders and be dependent on one," (I Thess. 4:12, NKJV); "Then the Lord said, "It is not good that the man should be alone; I will make him a helper fit for him," (Gen. 2:18, NKJV).

O. C. D.

OCD stands for obsessive compulsive disorder. This is basically, "A disorder in which people have recurring, unwanted thoughts, ideas, or sensations (obsessions) that make them feel driven to do something (compulsion), The repetitive behaviors, such as hand washing, checking on things or cleaning, can significantly interfere with a person's daily activities and social interactions. (American Psychiatric, www.psychiatry.org, and https://www.psychiatry. org/patients-families/ocd/what-is-obsessive-compulsive-disorderAccessed February 2, 2021).[54] People with OCD suffer from stressful thoughts and repetitive behaviors. They are addicted to such behaviors which if they do those behaviors, can cause great stress. OCD becomes a second to some people and becomes part of life. Whoever trusts in his own mind is a fool, but he who walks in wisdom will be delivered," (Proverbs 28:26, NKJV). "Obsessions are recurrent

---

[53] https://docs.google.com/document/d/1ORRkug4KmbcJq6wsiMkuZoe2wJGLNy4ESvnVjjfXsJc/edit, Accessed February 2, 2021.

[54] (American Psychiatric, www.psychiatry.org, and https://www.psychiatry.org/patients-families/ocd/what-is-obsessive-compulsive-disorderAccessed February 2, 2021).

and persistent thoughts, impulses, or images that cause distressing emotions such as anxiety or disgust. Many people with OCD recognize that the thoughts, impulses, or images are a product of their mind and are excessive or unreasonable... Compulsions are repetitive behaviors or mental acts that a person feels driven to perform in response to an obsession. The behaviors typically prevent or reduce a person's distress related to an obsession,"[55] Those who have OCD should be aware not to normalize their abnormality and think they are normal. They should try to avoid those behaviors to gravitate them and bit by bit eliminate the behaviors.

The Bible has many verses that God instructs us to desist from bad behaviors and to be self-controlled, "For God gave us a spirit not of fear but of power and love and self-control," (II Tim 1:7, NKJV); "Casting all your anxiety on him, because he cares for you," (I Peter 5:7, NKJV); "Therefore do not be anxious about tomorrow, for tomorrow will be anxious for itself. Sufficient for the day is its own trouble," (Matt. 6:34, NKJV); "In peace I will both lie down and sleep; for you alone, O LORD, make me dwell in safety," (Psalm 4:8, NKJV); "Fear not, for I am with you; do not be dismayed, for I am your God; I will help you, I will uphold you with my righteous hand," (Isaiah 41:10, NKJV); "Cast your burden on the LORD, and he will sustain you' he will never permit righteous to be moved," (Psalm 55:22, NKJV), "When the cares of my heart are many, your consolations clever my soul," (Psalm 94:19, NKJV), "Then the Lord knows how to rescue the godly from trials, and to keep the unrighteous under punishment until the day of judgement," (II Peter 2:9, NKJV), "Anxiety in a man's heart weighs him down, but a good makes him glad," (Proverbs 12:25, NKJV); "For God gave us a spirit of not fear but of power and love and self-control," (II Tim 1:7, NKJV).

Anxiety

Anxiety is being anxious about certain things or the uncertainty of things. Anxiety is "A mental health disorder characterized by feelings of worry, anxiety, or fear that are strong enough to interfere with one's daily activities... Examples of anxiety disorders include panic attacks, obsessive compulsive disorder, and post traumatic disorder,"[56] "Anxiety is a normal and often healthy emotion. However, when a person regularly feels disproportionate levels of anxiety, it might become a medical disorder. Anxiety disorders form a category of mental health diagnoses that lead to excessive nervousness, fear, apprehension, and worry," (Medical News Today, https://www.medicalnewstoday.com, Accessed February 2, 2021). Anxiety disorder includes social phobia, agoraphobia, phobias, and many disorders associated with anxiety. From a Biblical perspective, "anxiety" can affect Christians, but Paul advises that, "Do not be anxious

---

[55] Ibid.
[56] (Medical News Today, https://www.medicalnewstoday.com, Accessed February 2, 2021).

about anything, but in every situation, by prayer and petition, with thanksgiving, present your requests to God. And the peace of God, which transcends all understanding, will guard your hearts and your minds in Christ," (Phil.4:6-7, NKJV). When the anxiety becomes a focus point of your life and you don't trust God and depends on Him, becomes sins because you do not trust God but yourself.

The Bible has a lot of Scriptures that counsel those who have anxiety disorder. God counsels through His Word, "When anxiety was great within me, your consolation brought me joy," (Psalm 94:19, NKJV); "Do not let your hearts be troubled. Believe in God and believe in me," (John 14:1, NKJV); "For I am convinced that neither death nor life, neither angels nor demons, neither present nor the future, nor any powers, neither height nor depth, nor anything else in all creation, will be able to separate us from the love of God that is in Christ Jesus our Lord," (Romans 8:38-39, NKJV); "I sought the LORD, and He delivered answered me from all my fears," (Psalm 34:4, NKJV); "I want you to be free from anxieties," (I Cor. 7:32, NKJV); "Say to those who have an anxious heart, 'Be strong; fear not! Behold, your God will come with vengeance, with the recompense of God. He will come and save you," (Isaiah 35:4, NKJV); "When I am afraid, I put my trust in you," (Psalm 56:3, NKJV); "And which of you by being anxious can add a single hour to his span of life?" (Matt. 6:27, NKJV); "Casting all your anxieties on him, because he cares for you," (I Peter 5:7, NKJV); "Now may the Lord of peace himself always give you peace in every way. The Lord be with you," (II Thess. 3:16, NKJV); "Do not be anxious about anything, but in everything by prayer and supplication with thanksgiving let your requests be made known to God," (Phil. 4:6, NKJV), "Therefore do not be anxious about tomorrow, for tomorrow will be anxious for itself. Sufficient for the day is its own trouble," (Matt. 6:34, NKJV), "Anxiety in a man's heart weighs him down, but a good makes him glad," (Proverbs 12:25, NKJV); When the righteous cry for help, the LORD hears and delivers them out of all their troubles," (Psalm 34:17, NKJV).

Addiction

The Biblical perspective about addiction is that it is an idol. It is a way, temporarily, to feel good and only be concerned with your own desires. The cure for addiction is knowing and fearing the Lord. This must be Christ-centered because that is where healing power is found. "Knowing God's abiding love replaces the empty love that comes from these substances. Fearing God, seeking forgiveness, and truly repenting of our sins produces a transformation that breaks the chains of addiction," (Addictions A Banquet in the Grave – Edward T. Welch). Addiction is a condition whereby one is being addicted to such a substance, a thing or an activity and has become a psychological and physical habit that one is failing to stop which may result in harming the individual. According to American Society of Addiction Medicine, it is defined as, "Addiction is a complex, chronic brain condition influenced by genes and the environment that is characterized by substance use or compulsive actions that continue despite harmful consequences… This behavior causes problems for the individual or those around them. So instead of helping the person cope with situations or overcome problems, it tends to undermine these abilities."[57] Depending on the Holy Spirit and being filled and led by Him, helps to break away from any addition. God frees those who depend on Him. "Where the Spirit of God is, there is freedom," (II Cor. 3:17, NKJV). God has given us a free will. We choose whether to subject ourselves to bad habits and addictions (Rom.6:16-18, NKJV). Therefore, we have power given by God to control ourselves and avoid sinful behaviors, able to break away from bad habits and addictions.

Scott and Lambert assert, "Then, in a counseling session in February (we had begun counseling in October), Julie admitted that she had begun drinking daily resuming patterns of alcohol addiction that had been dormant for several years. She had grown up in a troubled home with two alcoholic parents and developed serious problems herself. Her drunkenness was doubly damaging-the problem of the alcohol itself and it was compounded by her mixing it with prescriptions."[58] Addiction becomes something one depends on to survive.

The information that I may need about this client to make an accurate diagnosis based on the DMS diagnosis criteria is about whether he drinks alcohol, or he is on legal drugs, his income, his religion if ever he has a religion and his past. As psychotherapist, they are some checklists I must employ in order to get as much information of the client as possible.

As a professional practitioner, I must know his limitations, but he must overcome those limitations by taking practical steps. Being respectful, developing good relationships, reading extensively about diverse cultures and religions, understanding people's ethical values in their own contexts and promoting healthy eating, exercise and education. In the case study, the mother shows a sense of resilience to make sure that her son is helped by the therapist. Although peers become more important during adolescence, it has been discovered that parents still have great influence on adolescent behavior (Burrow-Sanchez, J. J. 2006. p. 285. Para. 2). Some of the challenges of the adolescents is to discuss with them openly about the substance abuse. In the case study, the adolescent shows the signs of hallucination, intoxication, no control of thoughts, no balance, visionally impaired because of effects of either alcohol or drugs. The client in the case study can be diagnosed with psychiatric disorder and substance use disorder because of the behavioral patterns that he displaces without coherence and showing confusion in his speech. He shows the symptoms of withdrawal syndromes. He has substance abuse not dependence. The criteria for abuse and dependence shows variance with substance abuse. The substance uses prevalence, attitudes indicate a pattern of behavior. As an African American client, it is

---

[57] Stuart Scott and Heath Lambert, *Counseling the Hard Cases*, (Nashville: B & H Publishers), 2012, p. 266.
[58]

estimated that African Americans are diagnosed with psychosis and Latinos with depression with the symptoms of substance abuse, stemming from cultural, (Escobar, J. I., & Vega, W. A. 2006. p. 44. para. 5.)

Transference and Counter Transference when utilizing the Interpersonal Psychotherapy Approach

The discussion on transference and counter transference in interpersonal psychotherapy and the theoretical underpinnings related to transference and counter transference are crucial in understanding patient's dynamics.

Transference in therapy is a situation whereby the feelings, desires, anxiety, and concepts from another person are redirected and applied to another person to enhance therapeutic setting. The emotions and feelings that the client experienced during his/her childhood or with their teachers, parents, relatives, or someone who had influence in his/her life, especially negatively, then those feelings are directed to the therapist. Sigmund Freud developed the concept of countertransference to refer to a situation in which the psychologist's emotions, unconsciously, are transferred influenced by a person in therapy and the reaction by the psychologist is called countertransference (Good-Therapy, 2007). www.goodtherapy.org). Transference in interpersonal psychotherapy is where the feelings, emotions, desires and all the expectations of an individual are transferred and redirected to another person in a therapeutic setting to connect with the client in therapy. The good example is when one's parents were difficult to cope with because of their disciplines, chastisement, or time-out they were exposed to, these feelings can be redirected to client in therapy or vice versa. It is when one transfers the past feelings or emotions into the present situation.

The transference is usually unconscious redirecting of the feelings or emotions to a person, not intentionally. When one is young and older, when something is done to them especially, bad feelings or emotions, they are deposited into subconsciousness. When a certain situation or circumstance present itself, the subconscious pops up and reminds you of the similar circumstance and transference of those emotions or feelings start to kick in. In the same vein, counter transference is when the therapist transfers his/her emotions to the client who is in therapy which is usually because of transference during the treatment. It is very common for the therapist to do counter transference. It is fundamental for the therapist to take cognizance of not allowing counter transferences and transferences not to influence his/her principles and Interpersonal Psychotherapy code of conducts. The therapist can avoid the trap of counter transferences by identifying the spot feelings beneath anxieties. Kraemer alludes that his practical reasons to uphold countertransference as good and normal is that it actually exists because it is inevitable, according to many authors (Kraemer, W. P. p. 30. para. 2. 1958).

In the therapeutic setting, a client can direct and apply certain feelings and emotions to a therapist, unconsciously during therapeutic session. According to Kraemer's assertion, countertransference becomes part of the therapist's blind sport, and it cannot be dismissed in terms of bias. Both Jung and Freud emphasize making and controlling conscious contents. As a result, defense mechanism exhumed in subconscious of the client, can cause havoc on the client's mental health and in the interpersonal relationships. The clients most of the time make those transferences to the therapist in which they apply their emotions and feeling of someone in their lives in the past or present who might have influenced them in certain direction. Freud continues to hold on saying that both ego and shadow are accepted as essential counter parts in psychic wholeness (Ibid. 30. para. 2). Servedio brings another concept about transference. He propounds that transference in terms of communication cannot be one-sided proposition but both transference and countertransference are universal phenomenon, which is relevant in analytical setting, (Servedio E. 1956. p. 392) quoted by (Kraemer, 1958, p. 32. para. 1). In counter transference, in which the therapist's feelings and emotions are directed to the client, the therapist presents a case in which even if the case affectionate or hostile, can usher threats to treatment of the client if not managed appropriately. "The focus in psychodynamic psychotherapy is, in large part, the therapist and patient recognizing the transference relationship and exploring the relationship's meaning. Since the transference between patient and therapist happens on an unconscious level, psychodynamic therapists who are largely concerned with a patient's unconscious material use the transference to reveal unresolved conflicts patients have with childhood figures," (en.m. Wikipedia.org/wiki/Transference,), retrieved January 17, 2019.

The transference and countertransference are seen as integral part of interpersonal psychotherapy in the way. Transference is an indispensable element of analytical work that plays fundamental role in interpersonal psychotherapy. The analyst must take sides with the instincts and struggle against ego and its resistances which resist repetition, hence, opposes transference of instinctual impulses, (Racker, H., 1970. p. 15. para. 2). Transference was predominant, as resistance, but now it is considered the resisted and the rejected, (Ibid. p.15. para. 2). Transference and countertransference play important role in interpersonal psychotherapy approach as has proven to be effective to practice if the skills, techniques, and interventions are utilized and practiced properly. The Interpersonal therapy focuses on specific problem of the client and can reduce the symptoms and can create good relationships. To understand the client's unconscious impulses, resistance and transference through intuition, makes the therapist to understand unresolved conflicts reflected in the client (Ibid. p. 16. para. 3). It can enhance problem solving and increase communication skills needed to anchor relationships. These promote interpersonal awareness and learning, resulting in improved relational capacity and symptom reduction. The social learning processes promote both intrapersonal and interpersonal change and enhances communication skills (Anchin, 1982. p. 117. Para. 2).

The intuitive grasp is manifested through one's unconsciousness for self-assessment, (Racker, H. p. 17). Interpersonal psychotherapy comes with some challenges and limitations that the therapist should be aware of. When you are with the client in the process of therapy, the therapist must empathize with the client but sometimes the clients do not recognize one's empathy. Instead, they would attack you verbally. The therapist should be caring, non-judgmental, inspire hope, be able to repair ruptures and to find new ways that are better for the clients but sometimes the clients do not see the way out. The clients' conquering resistances and admitting the instinctual and emotional complexes which has the flashbacks from his past into his consciousness, impeded by unexpected phenomenon of the transference. Freud discovered that the analyst's work is like his, also that the impulses and feelings towards the client and Freud called this phenomenon countertransference (Racker, p.18. para. 2).

Ethical and Multicultural Self-Assessment

The importance of ethical and multicultural competency in the practice of professional psychology plays a pivotal role.

To be an ethical and multicultural competent professional psychology practitioner, one must have self-assessment to evaluate one's knowledge, skills, and attitudes on professional competencies to identify personal limitations. Ethical and multicultural competency is fundamental to a professional psychology practitioner because of the diversity and global village we live in, and one must be aware of other cultures, traditions, norms, religions. It does not mean that the practitioner must know the client's cultures deeply but just to be aware of, to acknowledge and to tolerate other people's cultures is fundamental. The professional psychology practitioner must know his/her limitations but must overcome those limitations by taking practical steps. Being respectful, developing good relationships, reading extensively about diverse cultures and religions, understanding people's ethical values in their own contexts, and promoting healthy eating, exercise, and education. "The balance may be achieved elegantly using cultural adaptation procedures. We define cultural adaptation as the systematic modification of an evidence-based treatment (EBT) or intervention protocol to consider language, culture, and context in such a way that it is compatible with the client's cultural patterns, meanings, and values," Bernal, G., Jiménez-Chaffey, M. I., & Domenech-Rodrígues, M. M. (2009). P. 261. The professional psychology practitioner ought to understand the matrix of cultures and ethical values of his/her patients/client as alluded by Bernal, Jimenez-Chafey, and Domenech-Rodrigues.

The demographic changes of the country pose some challenges to professional psychology practitioner, but those challenges have to be met head-on in order to bring about stability and professionalism in the field of psychology. "The delivery of ethical and culturally consistent therapeutic approaches has continued to challenge practitioners today because of demographic changes throughout the country, professional mandates, and the complex manner in which culture is understood and manifested therapeutically," Gallardo, M. E., Johnson, J., Parham, T. A., & Carter, J. A. (2009). p. 246. When demography changes in the society, so does the field of psychology changes to meet those challenges. When the country changes demographically, with diverse cultures, and influx population, history teaches that even knowledge, skills, attitudes change to meet the challenges from one generation to another. Cross-cultural misunderstanding between the providers and the patients can create negative underpinnings that can have lasting impacts in the lives of any given group of people. If the practitioner and the patient have different background, the language barrier, ethical values, interpretations, the medical history obtained may be distorted because of the misunderstanding.

The professional psychology practitioner can eliminate the prejudices by learning about the patients' cultural backgrounds, religions, diet, health practices, language, and ethical values. Assumptions about patients' race, ethnicity, culture, gender, social and language skills should change the paradigm of thinking of a practitioner to meet the needs. (Management Sciences for Health. (n.d.). The provider's guide to quality and culture: Quality and culture quiz. (Retrieved November 6, 2018, from http://academicdepartments.musc.edu/gme/pdfs/Quality). It is imperative to understand your audience/patients as a psychology practitioner to serve them well and to develop mutual relationships and respect. The five steps towards addressing the limitations to become more ethically and multiculturally competent are as follows:

1. **Awareness of practitioner's cultural values and biases** – The professional psychology practitioner must be aware of his/her cultural and ethical values or bias that can limit their professional practice. They must be ready to adjust to their cultural and racial biases to accommodate other human beings who have their cultures and ethical values.

2. **Awareness of client's worldview** – Professional psychology practitioner must be cognizance of his/her clients' worldview and acknowledge that they have different worldviews, different personalities, and be willing to adjust to aid the patients/clients.

3. **Cultural strategic interventions** – Once the professional psychology practitioner intentionally takes some steps to be culturally competent in discharging his/her professional duties, he/she becomes aware of the clients' beliefs, ethical values, religious views, and language. He/she becomes aware of the potential to be the best practitioner in the city, as he/she aims to transcends nationality, race, religion, beliefs, and prejudices of the clients. (Online Counseling Programs, (2017), 10 Multicultural Factors to Consider in Counseling, https://onlinecounselingprograms.com/blog/multicultural-counseling-model/).

4. **Cultural competence** – The professional psychology will be able to assimilate different behaviors, attitudes, skills, and knowledge, cross-culturally to embrace diversity. This will open the opportunities to impact the society. The cultural skilled practitioner also recognizes his/her limits to his/her competence and expertise.

5. **Cultural Relevance** – The professional psychology practitioner will try to be relevant with his/her patients/clients by revolving according to the needs of the clients/patients. Relevance is not complacent, but it is the realization of the changing times and intentionally, becoming congruent with the surrounding needs, situations, and circumstances around oneself.

The five steps address the limitations of a professional psychology practitioner to be ethically and multiculturally competent. To be ethically and multiculturally competent, it enhances the practitioner to gain the knowledge, awareness, beliefs, values, and practical skills of the diverse cultures, to value, respect and celebrate the diversity but also remaining true to him/herself as a person without losing what he/she is worth.

Critical thinking perspective and an analysis of the two articles, "Urinalysis" and "Vaccines May Fuel Autism Epidemic," highlight fundamental issues that reveal the growing concerns in the medical field and how to deal with the perceptions and solutions.

"Urinalysis," according to research has brought the inmates/parolees and the government staff some concerns and worries, especially the conducts, the process, the shame associated with the stigma and the results that do not substantiate the outcome as intended. "Urinalysis" procedures to detect heroin used by inmates/parolees has raised eyebrows in the manner it has been conducted. The tests to determine whether the person has ingested heroin to make informed decisions and whether the person had gone back to drugs, or whether the treatment is good for him/her. The mental health personnel are also concerned if the person need to be placed in the commitment facility. The researchers are also looking to see if the methods used are evidence-based and empirically credible.

Some concerns have been raised, especially on the procedures and the use of "Urinalysis" to detect the heroin in the human body. With all the tests, the article reveals that, "Later evidence indicates beyond dispute the inadequacy and inaccuracy results of the nalline test, and thus the prematurity of the court's uncritical hospitality to its results," Lithwick, D. (2002, July 3). Although the article also points out that such tests when conducted under laboratory conditions by first-class technicians possess a high degree of accuracy, Lithwick D. (2002). "Urinalysis" has been used by companies to detect their employees during their interviews and annually medical check-ups. The iron part of it is that the article indicates even the schools in the surrounding areas with high drugs use were now using "Urinalysis" which sounds like a fallacy report, thus the first error. The privacy of individuals is violated, and it is against the law to conduct research on people without their consents.

The second error that is detected in the article is the statement, "This paper is a preliminary statement attempting to examine some of the social scientific aspects of the urinalysis procedures in the detection of heroin use." "Attempting to examine" is a technical error in scholarly writing. Researchers do not claim about the "accuracy of tests under laboratory condition" in a dogmatic way as mentioned in page 304 of the article. The procedures of "urinalysis" became corrupt in Vietnam to gauge the dimensions of the drug problem in the American soldiers when money was paid secretly to change the results of the urinalysis. The staff who conducted the urinalysis procedures became so corrupt that they would accept apple juice samples in place of urine.

The third error was in the discrepancies between the number of respondents and the number of the reported responses in the testing of urinalysis, Table 1., page 305. The interview materials reveal specific character of the responses. There is no test reliability of Urinalysis of the accuracy under field condition. The fact is that there is no procedure available for cross-checking, page 305. Errors are always encountered because of different procedures administered, technicians' mistakes, and the drugs administered. The errors happen when, "Switching urines, using obfuscating drugs, removing preservatives from specimen bottles, leaving the cap of the bottle of specimen half open, diluting urine with water, producing specimens insufficient of quantity for chemical analysis and scheduling drug intake around the test," Lithwick, D. (2002, July 3), p. 306. For successful tests, adequate supervision must be administered with professionalism. The attitudes of both the respondents and the supervisors must be coordinated with intellectual praos for the results to be reliable and credible.

The implications of the errors which are made can discredit the credibility of urinalysis results, the discrepancies affect the authenticity of supervisors, corruption during the urinalysis procedures can put a dent on scientific and laboratory methods employed.

The "Vaccine May Fuel Autism Epidemic" article has some fundamental issues that need to be addressed without hesitation. Autistic children are being severely incapacitated with developmental disability that have no cure. For some decades now, the causes of autism remain unknown although they are some suggestions that child vaccines are the culprit. To substantiate the claim or hypothesis of increased cases of autism, thimerosal is at the top of the list which is being investigated although the evidence is inconclusive. "In 1999 the National Academy of Sciences Institute of Medicine (IOM) must have thought there was something seriously wrong when it supported removal of thimerosal from vaccines, stating that it was "a prudent measure in support of the public goal to reduce mercury exposure of infants and children as much as possible… It is no secret among government and health officials that mercury is toxic and causes serious adverse reactions," Kelly P. O'Meara, (2003, June 24), p. 24. Therefore, thimerosal and mercury must not be included in the vaccines for the children. It is bizarre, "toxicity of mercury and top U.S. health officials have called for its removal," O'Meara. Then the question is why is thimerosal and mercury are still in vaccines if it has been discovered that they cause autism to children?

The dilemma in confronting Food and Drug Administration is that they have very close ties to the pharmaceutical companies. Ethical issues versus medical issues come into play. Barbara Loe Fisher is founder of the National Vaccine Information Center, asserts, "There are many things in vaccines that could be causing these disorders, and thimerosal is only part of the problem. In the last 20 years, we have gone from giving children twenty-three doses of seven vaccines to thirty-eight doses of twelve vaccines," Barbara L. Fisher, quoted by O'Meara, (2003), 24.

The errors that have been committed are with all the vaccines with thimerosal and mercury to prevent diseases such as mumps, measles, malaria, asthma, chickenpox, diphtheria, tetanus, hepatitis, influenza, rubella etc., some epidemics have been created instead, such as autism. The implications and the impact of the side effects of the vaccines are huge. Children and their parents are battling the new diseases and epidemics that do not have any clue as to how they can overcome this epidemic as the scientific researchers are also perplexed with the emerging diseases and prevention associated with the vaccines that cause autism.

Analysis of Two Articles "Sadder and Accurate, False Memory for Negative Material in Depression" and "Reduced Positive Memory biases in remitted depression."

An analysis of the two professional articles on "Sadder and Accurate, False Memory for Negative Material in Depression" to contradict the statement of the original article with a different view from another article, "Reduced Positive Memory biases in remitted depression."

Mood and emotion states usually affect the memory of an individual. "Understanding this complex interaction of mood and memory is important, given its critical role in emotion regulation and emotional disorders," Joormann, Teachman, and Gotlib, (2009), Sadder and Less Accurate? False Memory for Negative Material in Depression. There is individual mood-memory congruent. It is asserted, "First, difficulties in cognitive control (i.e., focal attention to relevant stimuli and inhibition of irrelevant material) result in memory deficits for non-emotional material…" Ibid. p. 412. The research has revealed that there is evidence that indicate that the depressed memory is found in unstructured memory. "These results suggest that, at least with respect to memory deficits, depressed people might have the ability to perform at the level of non-depressed people in structured situations but have problems doing this in unconstrained situations (Hertel, 2004)," (Ibid. 412). Depressed people fluctuate in moods and emotions hence affect and impair their memory and judgment. Their attention which is their cognitive control result in memory deficits.

"Negative affect associated with depressive disorders makes mood-congruent material more accessible and mood- incongruent material less accessible, a finding that is consistent with predictions from schema and network theories of emotions," Ibid. 412. The article further alludes, "In a meta- analysis of studies assessing recall performance, Matt et al. (1992) found that people with major depression remember 10% more negative than positive words. Non-depressed control participants, in contrast, demonstrated a memory bias for positive information in 20 of 25 studies... It is important to note that the effects of mood on memory may help explain why depressed people are caught in a vicious cycle of increasingly negative mood and enhanced accessibility of negative material that maintains or exacerbates negative affect and hinders emotion regulation," Ibid. 412-413. It is absurd to realize that in the article, the authors assert that they are different errors in memory. One of the areas of errors is whereby individuals can forget stimuli, "People can forget stimuli that they have seen, and they can "remember" items that they have not seen. This latter error, often termed a "commission error" or "false memory," has rarely been investigated in depression. Results of research examining mood and memory in nonclinical samples and findings from studies of mood-congruent biases in depressed samples lead to different predictions regarding the production of false memories in major depressive disorder (MDD)." Ibid. 413.

The article presented a study that was designed to investigate and observe if clinical depression is related with the false emotional material.

The present study was designed to investigate whether clinical depression is associated with increased false recall of neutral and/or emotional material. Compared with control participants, depressed participants falsely recalled a higher proportion of negative lures. It is important to note that no group differences were obtained for recall of positive and neutral lures, indicating that the higher propensity for false recall in depression does not reflect a general deficit but, instead, is specific to the processing of negative material. Depressed participants also demonstrated less accurate recall than did their non-depressed counterparts for previously presented items, especially those from the positive lists, Ibid. 415.

The study or the research of the article did not bring credible evidence that clinical depression is related to false recall of neutral or emotional material. "The present findings suggest that the effects of clinically significant depression are quite different from those of induced mood," Ibid. 415. The conclusive analysis of the article is that it has biased opinions and errors bend to justify the research. Although the parts of the article contain valid and true analysis of the clinical depression and emotional material, but it does not produce evidence-based research.

In contrast to the article, "Sadder and Accurate? False Memory for Negative Material in Depression" the article by six authors, Githin J, Lythe K, Workman C, Moll J, Zahn R, entitled,

"European Psychiatry: Early Life Stress Explains Reduced Positive Memory Biases in Remitted Depression," presents contradictory assertion. The authors of this article argue, "There is contradictory evidence regarding negative memory biases in major depressive disorder (MDD) and whether these persist into remission, which would suggest their role as vulnerability traits rather than correlates of mood state," Githin J, Lythe K, Workman C, Moll J, Zahn R, (2017). The article dispels the hypothesis of "False Memory for Negative Material in Depression" presented by Joormann, Teachman, and Gotlib, (2009). The contradictory assertions point out further that, Early life stress (ELS), common in patients with psychiatric disorders, has independently been associated with memory biases, and confounds MDD versus control group comparisons. Furthermore, in most studies negative biases could have resulted from executive impairments rather than memory difficulties per se," Ibid. 59. The argument against the "False Memory for Negative Material" is substantiated by the analogy that their contradictory evidence patterning to the negative memory biases.

The results of a conducted research revealed that there is a tendency of reduced biases towards memory for positive. "Only MDD patients with ELS showed a reduced bias (accuracy/speed ratio) towards memory for positive vs. negative materials when compared with MDD without ELS and with HC participants; attenuated positive biases correlated with number of past major depressive episodes, but not current symptoms. They were no biases towards self-blaming or self-praising memories," Ibid. 59. The results showed that they were very limited biases. Therefore, "This demonstrates that reduced positive biases in associative memory were specific to MDD patients with ELS rather than a general feature of MDD and were associated with lifetime recurrence risk which may reflect a scarring effect. If replicated, our results would call for stratifying MDD patients by history of ELS when assessing and treating emotional memories," Ibid. 60. The article defends the assertion that the mood and emotional is not always affected by the memory of individuals.

The article defends most of the argument presented by "Sadder Accurate? False Memory for Negative Material in Depression." "Given the close link between memories and mood postulated by Bower, one could postulate that the reduced positive memory biases sometimes reported in MDD contribute to the reductions in positive affect predicted to be specific to MDD by the decreased positive emotionality model of MDD... To our knowledge, self-blame-related memory biases have not been investigated in MDD, and the literature on the importance of self-reference effects when encoding emotional materials in mediating emotional memory biases in MDD is inconsistent." Ibid. 61. It is imperative to refute the claim by the first article contending that the people with major depression remember 10% more negative than positive words. "We tested the alternative predictions of the self-blaming bias and positive emotionality models of vulnerability to MDD on associative memory for temporal and situational context. We favored the hypothesis that MDD patients would show self-blame-selective rather than negative or positive emotion-selective changes in associative memory compared to a healthy control (HC) group," Ibid.

Applying critical thinking to reading of psychological research and professional literature allows one to employ scholarly analysis of every book, article, journal, or any research presented. It gives one confidence and credibility to be able to discharge professional skills in the academic field to be able to assess, evaluate, and authenticate if the material one is reading is credible and with verifiable and strong sources.

Case Study – Personality Disorder

The discussion of DSM diagnosis of the client in the case study and the rationale for assigning the diagnosis based on the DSM. People with personality disorder suffer isolation and loneliness because of the personal limitations that they have. "Clinicians frequently encounter depressed patients experiencing panic or patients of schizophrenia with varying degrees of impairment or a patient exhibiting symptoms of anxiety that could not be clearly labeled as abnormal," (American Psychiatric Association. 2013. p.16).

The DSM diagnosis of the client in the case of loneliness and anxiety disorder. The client in the case study, assigning him to the DSM schizophrenia cannot be ruled out although it might be an acute schizophrenia. Related to that, the client may be suffering from Post Stress Traumatic Disorder (PSTD). He suffered from emotional and verbal abuse from his father. The pattern of behavior has a long history of his relationship with his classmates at college whom he scorned during that time they were together.

As a result of isolation, loneliness, paranoia, insomnia, he has developed defensive mechanism to spend most his free time playing online games, distancing himself from other people. Even his mother annoys him. The client is experiencing florid symptoms. The dimensional approach of DSM diagnosis has been discovered that it helps and chart the course of the disorder, which ultimately, distinguishes between normal and abnormal, thus it can be used to screen for mental disorders, (Nussbaum. APA, 2013, p. 16).

The rationale for assigning the client with anxiety disorder and schizophrenia is developing of the personality disorder showing in his behavior pattern, which is not consistence, and in the process, he consumed by himself, and he mentions that he does not need any friends at all. He does not have friends, spends most his free time gaming online. He has shut down everyone except his mother. He is paranoid and cannot trust anyone. During his school days, he was focused on making to the Dean's list, not in socializing with other students. As a psychotherapist, it is not easy to accurately diagnose a client using DMS diagnosis criteria. It is imperative to learn that even Liebermann and Thomas Insel issued a joint statement, pointing out that the criteria used in clinical practice to diagnose DMS may not offer the credible answers according to the research, "…Looking forward, laying the groundwork for a future diagnostic system that more directly reflects modern brain science will require openness to rethinking traditional categories. It is increasingly evident that mental illness will be best understood as disorders of brain structure and function that implicate specific domains of cognition, emotion, and behavior." (Liebermann and Insel, 2013). This is a strong statement from then the President of the APA and his colleague to make such observation.

The information that I may need about this client to make an accurate diagnosis based on the DMS diagnosis criteria is about whether he drinks alcohol, on drugs, his income, his religion if ever he has a religion and his past. As psychotherapist, they are some checklists I must employ to get as much information the client as possible.

The professional practitioner must know his/her limitations but must overcome those limitations by taking practical steps. Being respectful, developing good relationships, reading extensively about diverse cultures and religions, understanding people's ethical values in their own contexts and promoting healthy eating, exercise and education. "The balance may be achieved elegantly with cultural adaptation procedures. We define cultural adaptation as the systematic modification of an evidence-based treatment (EBT) or intervention protocol to consider language, culture, and context in such a way that it is compatible with the client's cultural patterns, meanings, and values," Bernal, G., Jiménez-Chafey, M. I., & Domenech-Rodrígues, M. M. (2009). P. 261. The professional psychology practitioner ought to understand the matrix of cultures and ethical values of his/her patients/client as alluded by Bernal, Jimenez-Chafey, and Domenech-Rodrigues.

"The delivery of ethical and culturally consistent therapeutic approaches has continued to challenge practitioners today because of demographic changes throughout the country, professional mandates, and the complex manner in which culture is understood and manifested therapeutically," Gallardo, M. E., Johnson, J., Parham, T. A., & Carter, J. A. (2009). p. 246. When demography changes in the society, so does the field of psychology changes to meet those challenges. Cross-cultural misunderstanding between the providers and the patients can create negative underpinnings that can have lasting impacts in the lives of any given group of people. If the practitioner and the patient have different background, the language barrier, ethical values, interpretations, the medical history obtained may be distorted because of the misunderstanding.

Clinical Psychology in Context

Strengths and Limitations of the Interpersonal Psychology Approach

Interpersonal Psychotherapy approach to practice as a clinical profession brings new perspective and a new dimension in the field. Interpersonal psychotherapy approach has proven to be effective to practice if the skills, techniques, and interventions are utilized and practice. "In highlighting both the covert and overt levels of these relational phenomena and their reciprocity, the interpersonal approach also provides a framework for seamlessly integrating concepts and techniques associated with other treatment approaches to PDs" (Anchin, 1982a, 1982b, 2002; Pincus & Cain, 2008, p. 113. Para. 2). The Interpersonal therapy focuses on specific problem of the client and can reduce the symptoms and can create good relationships. It can enhance problem solving and increase communication skills needed to anchor relationships. These promote interpersonal awareness and learning, resulting in improved relational capacity and symptom reduction. The social learning processes promote both intrapersonal and interpersonal change and enhances communication skill (Anchin, 1982. p. 117. Para. 2).

Transference in therapy is a situation whereby the feelings, desires, anxiety, and concepts from another person are redirected and applied to another person to enhance therapeutic setting. The emotions and feelings that the client experienced during his/her childhood or with their teachers, parents, relatives, or someone who had influence in his/her life, especially negatively, then those feelings are directed to the therapist. Interpersonal Psychology approach to practice presents both benefits as well challenges. The benefits for using interpersonal psychology approach are that it helps to identify problems expressed in emotions, learning skills to foster good rapport, and it focuses on specific problem areas that need to be addressed. It can assist to solve problems, conflicts, disputes thus improve the therapist's skills of communication by addressing issues such as depression, anxiety, and be able administer treatment and symptoms for social adjustment for clients.

The other benefits for interpersonal psychotherapy approach are that it strengthens relationships that can serve as support network for the benefit of the therapist. "Across all therapeutic modalities, nothing predicts good outcome as reliably as the patient's experience of the therapist as warm, caring, and genuine, and, thus, the patient's experience of being seen, understood and helped," (Safran, J. D., & Muran, J. C. (2000). Interpersonal Psychotherapy approach creates symbiotic relationship with the client if it is done with empathy and professionalism. It is a type of therapy structured model for treating of mental health issues which is timely in the process it improves the interpersonal relationships. It is a brief or a short-structured therapy that produce immediate results. Transference and countertransference play important role in interpersonal psychotherapy approach as has proven to be effective to practice if the skills, techniques, and interventions are utilized and practiced properly.

The Interpersonal therapy focuses on specific problem of the client and can reduce the symptoms and can create good relationships. To understand the client's unconscious impulses, resistance, and transference through intuition, makes the therapist to understand unresolved conflicts reflected in the client (Ibid. p. 16. para. 3). It can enhance problem solving and increase communication skills needed to anchor relationships. These promote interpersonal awareness and learning, resulting in improved relational capacity and symptom reduction. The social learning processes promote both intrapersonal and interpersonal change and enhances communication skill (Anchin, 1982. p. 117. Para. 2). The therapist should be caring, non-judgmental, inspire hope, be able to repair ruptures and to find new ways that are better for the clients but sometimes the clients do not see the way out. The clients' conquering resistances and admitting the instinctual and emotional complexes which has the flashbacks from his past into his consciousness, impeded by unexpected phenomenon of the transference. Interpersonal Psychotherapy approach is very fundamental in assessing, evaluating, assigning the clients with DSM-criteria, and applying practical treatment.

Medical Condition and Psychological Diagnosis

It is the responsibility and the duty of the psychologist to diagnose and address the symptoms of the patient's pathology disorder or condition disorder accurately, bearing in mind that if the psychologist misdiagnoses, the repercussions for the psychologist and for the client are huge. There is a difference between medical condition and psychological disorder. Medical condition is an unhealthy state of a client whereas psychology condition is mental disorder or psychiatric disorder which may create stress, depression, bipolar, (American Psychiatric Association. (2013). The patterns of behavioral disorders come with symptoms that the psychologist must observe and be able to ascertain the therapy method for the client.

Another diagnostic consideration includes physical symptoms such as stress, headaches, anxiety, depression. Neurological symptoms are the signs of early brain tumors because of intracranial pressure. Medical conditions may mimic psychological disorder and the psychologist should be able to assess, diagnosis and treat the client appropriately, (Bondi, M. W. 1992, p. 307. Para. 8). The two ways to minimize instances of diagnosis is by using DSM criteria and avoiding cultural and gender biases. Diagnosis of a client's illness has several factors to be taken into consideration. Culture is one of the factors to be considered when diagnosing a client, including validation of the client's sickness. It provides tools to be applied after a diagnosis, and it allows the psychotherapist to plan for the treatment, (Paris, J., 2015, p. 17). The DSM is relative to culture, familial norms, values, and social backgrounds and both the client and the therapist should work out a strategy to find a common ground to discuss and find a solution to the problems.

It is therefore, imperative for clinical psychologists to follow set up criteria outlined in DSM for accurate diagnosis because the goal is to have accurate diagnosis and for effective treatment. The classification system of the DSM in making a diagnosis requires robust analysis of the strengths and limitations. If I suspect a medical condition, I will use ethical and professional skills. I must assess, diagnose, and apply treatment according to psychology ethical code of conduct and use my discretion as a professional clinician.

Clinical Psychology on Human Health

Personality Disorder and Current Controversies

Culture and gender have important roles in the client's influence when it comes to diagnosis of personality disorder. Diagnosis of a client's illness has a few factors to be taken into consideration. Culture is one of the factors to be considered when diagnosing a client, including validation of the client's sickness. It provides tools to be applied after a diagnosis, and it allows the psychotherapist to plan for the treatment, (Paris, J., 2015, p. 17). Gender also plays a fundamental role when diagnosing a client because every client in any given culture needs to be respected and treated with every respect and dignity. Diagnosis is defined as, "A personality disorder is an enduring pattern of inner experience and behavior that deviates markedly from the expectations of one's culture, is pervasive and inflexible, has an onset in adolescence or early adulthood, is stable over time, and leads to distress or impairment" (APA, 2013, p. 645).

Ethical and multicultural competency is fundamental to a professional psychology practitioner because of the diversity and global village we live in and one has to be aware of other cultures, traditions, norms, religions. It does not mean that the practitioner must know the client's cultures deeply or well but there is a need to be aware, have a knowledge of your client and to tolerate other people's cultures. The world today has become a global village and it is inevitable to have clients from all walks of live with different culture from yours. Being respectful, developing good relationships, reading extensively about diverse cultures and religions, understanding people's ethical values in their own contexts, and promoting healthy eating, exercise and education is the key. "The balance may be achieved elegantly using cultural adaptation procedures. We define cultural adaptation as the systematic modification of an evidence-based treatment (EBT) or intervention protocol to consider language, culture, and context in such a way that it is compatible with the client's cultural patterns, meanings, and values," (Bernal, G., et al, 2009. P. 261).

The controversy associated with the diagnosis of women with borderline personality disorder is aimed at determining if ever they are biases towards women in personality disorder diagnosis. The clinician's role was conducted using Bem Sex Role Inventory-Short Form and the results confirmed that there are biases towards women. Patient's sex, especially women, had a direct effect when the research was conducted (Crosby, J, P., and Sprock, J. 20104, p. 583). "However, it was noted that more men are diagnosed with antisocial, and possibly obsessive-compulsive, paranoid, schizoid, and schizotypal personality disorders," (Ibid. p.584). The conclusive analysis is that there is bias towards women when it comes to borderline personality disorder diagnosis. Research has indicated that clinicians assign different personality disorder diagnosis based on client's sex and the clinicians have such biases which raises some concerns among clinicians (Ibid. p. 584. Para. 2).

Critical Thinking: Use of hypnosis in therapy

1. **McCann B., and Landers S., (2010), Hypnosis in the Treatment of Depression: Considerations in Research Designs and Methods, HHS Public Access, Apr. (2), 147-164. URL: https://www.ncbi.nlm.nih.gov/pmc/articles/PMC2856099/**

There is a deeply divided scholarly debate culminating from the evidenced-based treatment of depression using depressants in therapy or interpersonal psychotherapy. "In the United States, psychopharmacological approaches and certain forms of psychotherapy, particularly cognitive behavior therapy (CBT) and interpersonal psychotherapy (IPT) are generally recommended as treatments of choice for depression," McCann B., and Landers S., (2010), Hypnosis in the Treatment of Depression: Considerations in Research Designs and Methods, HHS Public Access, Apr. (2), 147-164. The article alludes that the empirically, validated treatment using antidepressant can also treat major psychiatric disorders. "Types of research support deemed appropriate for determining whether a particular form of psychotherapy has solid footing as evidence-based have been delineated by a task force of the American Psychological Association (APA), Ibid. Despite the conclusion that cognitive Behavioral Therapy (CBT) from meta-analysis indicated that it was superior treatment for depression, the research indicates that they are no forms of therapy that is above or superior to the other therapies but that they are all equally important in their own context for different patients. "In fact, there was a slight advantage for interpersonal psychotherapy, and nondirective supportive psychotherapy was somewhat less efficacious," McCann and Landers (2010).

In the context of hypnosis treatment of depression, Yapko proposes that, "hypnosis has relevance to the treatment of depression because hypnosis can help build positive expectancy regarding treatment, address numerous depressive symptoms (including insomnia and rumination), and modify patterns of self-organization (such as cognitive, response, attentional, and perceptual styles) that contribute to depressed thinking and mood" Michael Yapko (editor), in McCann and Lander (2010). They are some other approaches to use hypnosis to treat depression such as retrieval of past positive experience, the development of copying skills, augmenting interpersonal psychotherapy, and enhancing cognitive behavior therapy, McCann and Landers, (20100), https://www.ncbi.nlm.nih.gov/pmc/articles/PMC2856099/#R48. The clinicians are reluctant to use hypnosis to treat patients because the research concluded that

Dr. Sabelo Sam Gasela Mhlanga

hypnosis treatment of depression is harmful to some individuals. "We now turn to a description of several research methodologies and their suitability for exploring the treatment of depression using hypnotic methods. The first of these, the randomized controlled trial (RCT), is the current "gold standard" for empirically supported treatments (ESTs) and is a resource-intense methodology generally best suited to research settings. Two additional methods, single-case design and benchmarking are methods that can be more readily implemented within a clinical practice setting and may address some of the shortcomings of RCT approaches," McCann and Lander, (2010). The research reveals that the hypnosis does not authenticate the hypnosis as a treatment of depression to certain individuals because of its nature and whether hypnosis is a useful therapeutic strategy in treating depression.

2. **Syrjala K., Cummings C., and Donaldson G., (1992), Hypnosis or cognitive behavioral training for the reduction of pain and nausea during cancer treatment: a controlled clinical trial, Vol. 48. Issue 2. Feb., pp. 137-146.**

The second article is a hypnosis for the reduction of pain during cancer treatment. It is deemed a controlled clinical trial. "Few controlled clinical trials have tested the efficacy of psychological techniques for reducing cancer pain or post-chemotherapy nausea and emesis. In this study, 67 bone marrow transplant patients with hematological malignancies were randomly assigned to one of four groups prior to beginning transplantation conditioning... Patients completed measures of physical functioning (Sickness Impact Profile; SIP) and psychological functioning (Brief Symptom Inventory; BSI), which were used as covariates in the analyses," Syrjala K., Cumming C., Donaldson G., (1992). After the hypnosis treatment, the controlled clinical trial, as contended, "Analyses of the principal study variables indicated that hypnosis was effective in reducing reported oral pain for patients undergoing marrow transplantation. Risk, SIP, and BSI pre-transplant were found to be effective predictors of inpatient physical symptoms. Nausea, emesis, and opioid use did not differ significantly between the treatment groups," Syrjala, Cummings, and Donaldson, 137-146. They were some successes in the hypnosis for reducing pain on the 67 patients going through cancer retreatment although it cannot be substantiated to every patient.

The fallacies in the first article is that "psychopharmacological approaches and certain forms of psychotherapy, particularly cognitive behavior therapy (CBT) and interpersonal psychotherapy (IPT) are generally recommended as treatments of choice for depression," McCann B., and Landers S., (2010). The controversy that the hypnosis present is treating depression which has been delineated by a task force of the American Psychological Association (APA). They are seen as harmful to some individual as treatments. Although the research confirms that antidepressant can treat major psychiatric disorders, they are deemed harmful to others. The impact is that between two hypnoses, people are left confused as to which one is better treatment. i.e., cognitive behavior therapy (CBT) and interpersonal psychotherapy (IPT). The errors can be corrected by conducting a fair and credible research and trials using evidence-based tests.

In the second article, the fallacies are left glaring, although "Few controlled clinical trials have tested the efficacy of psychological techniques for reducing cancer pain or post-chemotherapy nausea and emesis," Syrjala, Cumming, and Donaldson (1992). Some researchers still doubt if the treatment is credible and effective. They say that the side effects weigh far more than the benefits. The fallacies can be examined, and then comprehensive approaches and research employed that can produce credible results in order to help those who are in pain because of cancer or chemotherapy. The research, trials, and evidence-based clinical tests can produce positive results to determine whether the medications are helpful or not.

The Impacts and Effects of Clinical Psychology on Human Health:

Mood Disorders and the Client

The assigned diagnosis of the client is mood disorder, anxiety disorder, personality disorder also referred to as borderline personality disorder. Borderline personality disorder has new markers to determine and evaluate the diagnosis. To evaluate borderline mental disorders effectively, the use of new EEG signal markers, values of the first and second kind errors are used. (Tychkov. A. V., Churakon. P.P., Alimuradov. A. K., et al, 2018). Assigning a client based on DSM is to accurately, diagnosis the client with the mental illness he/she suffers from. The client shows a sign of delusion disorder, and she meets the criteria for bipolar I because they are psychotic features with suicidal risks. They are also some major depressive episodes in the client's pattern of behavior, (Paris. J., 2015).

The client has suffered a number of things such as experience of sex with her husband that did not go well many times in her marriage. She says her husband told her that she was not intimate enough and then she developed low self-esteem. It resulted into a divorce medical insurance. She then narrates the sexual encounter with her two college colleagues whom she had sex with, but she could not tell whether it was a rape case, or she had consent with them. The client is not sure about her sexual orientation. She feels rejected, sad, depressed and as a result, she conceals her depression, frustration, and despondency. She then developed depressive episodes.

When she alludes to the fact that she believes that she does not have anyone that she can connect with, indicates that she really has come to the end of the road. She said that she feels worthless, hopeless and without a future. The client claims that she is left with one thing, i.e., the details of suicide. She says the suicide will be quick and painless, however, she has not figured it out the day she will do it.

According to DSM, the client has indeed, suicidal thoughts and she must be taken seriously. The therapist should never play down or minimize the claim of the client about her/his intentions to commit suicide. The client has indicated that she wants to commit suicide and sessions for psychotherapy and counseling need to be administered immediately, without delay because she has already planned her action. Although she may be seeking attention, any client who mentions about suicide must be assigned with the diagnosis and help should be given.

Interpersonal Psychology approach to practice presents both benefits as well as challenges. The benefits for using interpersonal psychology approach are that it helps to identify problems expressed in emotions, learning skills to foster good rapport, and it focuses on specific problem areas that need to be addressed. It can assist to solve problems, conflicts, disputes thus improving the therapist's skills of communication by addressing issues such as depression, anxiety, and be able to administer treatment and symptoms for social adjustment for clients. The other benefits for interpersonal psychotherapy approach are that it strengthens relationships that can serve as support network for the benefit of the therapist. "Across all therapeutic modalities, nothing predicts good outcome as reliably as the patient's experience of the therapist as warm, caring, and genuine, and, thus, the patient's experience of being seen, understood and helped," (Safran, J. D., & Muran, J. C. (2000). Interpersonal Psychotherapy approach creates symbiotic relationship with the client if it is done with empathy and professionalism.

Interpersonal psychotherapy comes with some challenges and limitations that the therapist should be aware of. When you are with the client in the process of therapy, the therapist must empathize with the client but sometimes the clients do not recognize one's empathy. Instead, they would attack you verbally. The therapist should be caring, non-judgmental, inspire hope, be able to repair ruptures and to find new ways that are better for the clients but sometimes the clients do not see the way out (American Psychological Association (Producer). (2009). The challenges and limitations for the therapists is to guide the clients so that they find solutions to their predicaments.

The cultures of the clients play importable roles in determining the types of therapy to administer. The challenges of the therapists with regards to cultures of their clients is to understand the cultures fully. Their belief systems, cultures, traditions, norms, ethics, religions, and family can be a big challenge to the therapists. Therefore, to contextualize the clients' cultures may be challenging experience, (APA, 2009. Gender issues can be a challenge for the therapists. Some clients lean to certain sexual orientations, and it becomes extremely hard to discuss gender disparities when they do not believe in certain sextual orientations of other people that they love. Even if the therapist does not believe in certain sexual orientations, he/

she should go beyond his/her belief systems. The therapist should create security for the clients, and sometimes it is challenging to convince the clients.

Interpersonal Psychotherapy

Interpersonal psychotherapy approach has proven to be effective to practice if the skills, techniques, and interventions are utilized and practice. "In highlighting both the covert and overt levels of these relational phenomena and their reciprocity, the interpersonal approach also provides a framework for seamlessly integrating concepts and techniques associated with other treatment approaches to PDs" (Anchin, 1982a, 1982b, 2002; Pincus & Cain, 2008, p. 113. Para. 2). The Interpersonal therapy focuses on specific problem of the client and can reduce the symptoms and can create good relationships. It can enhance problem solving and increase communication skills needed to anchor relationships. These promote interpersonal awareness and learning, resulting in improved relational capacity and symptom reduction. The social learning processes promote both intrapersonal and interpersonal change and enhances communication skill (Anchin, 1982. p. 117. Para. 2).

Interpersonal Psychology approach to practice presents both benefits as well as challenges. The benefits for using interpersonal psychology approach are that it helps to identify problems expressed in emotions, learning skills to foster good rapport, and it focuses on specific problem areas that need to be addressed. It can assist to solve problems, conflicts, disputes thus improve the therapist's skills of communication by addressing issues such as depression, anxiety, and be able to administer treatment and symptoms for social adjustment for clients. The other benefits for interpersonal psychotherapy approach is that it strengthens relationships that can serve as support network for the benefit of the therapist. "Across all therapeutic modalities, nothing predicts good outcome as reliably as the patient's experience of the therapist as warm, caring, and genuine, and, thus, the patient's experience of being seen, understood and helped," (Safran, J. D., & Muran, J. C. (2000). Interpersonal Psychotherapy approach creates symbiotic relationship with the client if it is done with empathy and professionalism. It is a type of therapy structured model for treating of mental health issues which is timely in the process it improves the interpersonal relationships. It is a brief or a short-structured therapy that produce immediate results.

Interpersonal psychotherapy comes with some challenges and limitations that the therapist should be aware of. When you are with the client in the process of therapy, the therapist must empathize with the client but sometimes the clients do not recognize one's empathy. Instead, they would attack you verbally. The therapist should be caring, non-judgmental, inspire hope, be able to repair ruptures and to find new ways that are better for the clients but sometimes the clients do not see the way out (American Psychological Association (Producer), (2009).

The challenges and limitations for the therapists is to guide the clients it sometimes becomes surmountable. It can also enhance active and non-judgmental treatment that address depression, grief and anxiety disorder, bipolar and social phobia.

The cultures of the clients play important roles in determining the types of therapy to administer. The challenges of the therapists with regards to cultures of their clients is to understand the cultures fully. Their belief systems, cultures, traditions, norms, ethics, religions, and family can be a big challenge to the therapists. Therefore, to contextualize the clients' cultures may be challenging experience, (APA, 2009. Gender issues can be a challenge for the therapists. Some clients lean to certain sexual orientations, and it becomes extremely hard to discuss gender disparities when they do not believe in certain sextual orientations of other people that they love. Even if the therapist does not believe in certain sexual orientations, he/she should go beyond his/her belief systems. The therapist should create security for the clients, and sometimes it is challenging to convince the clients. In the same vein, the client in IPT must be willing to make some changes in their life for the therapy to be effective because the therapeutic process is client motivated and driven. It is client centered and with disparity of populations and cultural differences, to some cultures the IPT works perfect but to some cultures it does not.

Psychodynamic/Object Relation Therapy

This is another branch of therapy of psychodynamic thought which focuses on relationships for personality. It was founded by Greenberg and Michell 1983.

Behavioral Therapy

This type of therapy focuses on ways to change behavioral relations and patterns that usually causes distress. It does not focus on unconscious reasons for a behavior. It focuses on personal current issues and situations to change them for the better for the person.

Cognitive Behavioral Therapy

This type of therapy is focused on psycho-social intervention aiming to reduce the symptoms of various condition, especially, depression and the anxiety disorders. The thoughts, beliefs and attitudes can distort human behavior, but it can be treated by recognizing and changing those harmful and troubling thought patterns which affect behaviors and emotions.

Clinical Eclective Therapy

The therapy is a flexible and multifaced approach and it allows the therapist to use effective methods that can address the client's needs. It is also referred to as a multi model or integrative therapy and uses various techniques.

Gottman/Marriage Therapy

This type of therapy focuses on improving the health of marriage and restoring romantic partnership within married couples. Basically, Gottman method of therapy is designed to disarm or reduce painful verbal communication between married couple. It equips couples with tools to enhance their affection to each other. It intentionally, breaks down the barriers to couples who may be facing negative challenges in their marriage.

EMDR Therapy

(Eye Movement Desensitization and Reprocessing), is a psychotherapy which assist people to experience healing of distress. It is designed and structured to encourage and allows patients to focus on the traumatic memories (Shapiro, 2001).

Social Skills Training Therapy

This type of behavioral therapy is utilizing social skills in people with mental disorders of developmental disabilities. This kind of therapy can be used to the teachers, therapists, and other professionals for training. A patient is led and encouraged to focus on teachable moments to enhance communication and social integration in order deal with mental disorders.

Dialective Behavioral Therapy

This type of therapy is evidence-based psychotherapy and endeavors to treat personal disorders and conflicts. The type of therapy focusing on treating mood disorders and suicidal ideation. If a patient is made to believe that he/she can change behavioral patterns such as self-harm and substance abuse can change their lives for the better. A patient can learn more about the things that trigger their emotional and cognitive regulation.

Group Therapy

This type of psychotherapy is centered on a particular topic. The purpose of Group Therapy is to create a good environment for counseling and treatments for patients' psychological disorders.

Matters of Mind: Psychotic Disorders & Schizophrenia Disorders

Psychotic and schizophrenia disorders have been seen as the most complicated and challenging diagnosis in the DSM. For example, the symptoms of psychotic disorder can be detected clearly and simply to some clients, while to some clients it is a bit difficult to observe. Fujii and Ahmed reiterate the hypothesis when they propound that the presentation of psychosis symptoms, the appearance of psychosis is often unexpected or puzzling (Fujii and Ahamed, 2002, p. 33. para. 1) "The disorder has conceptual relevance to understanding schizophrenia spectrum disorders" (Fujii and Ahmed, 2001. p. 33). Fujii and Ahmed (2002a) in their article, reported several potentially discriminating variables between PSTBI and schizophrenia to clients. Patients with PSTBI appear to have fewer negative symptoms. It is interesting to note Ahmed and Fujii (1998) argued that the DSM-IV criteria for PSTBI are inadequate, as they do not provide guidance to determine whether psychotic symptoms are a direct physiological consequence of a previous head injury, or to aid in differential diagnosis (Fujii D. 2002, p. 33. p. para. 14).

Schizophrenia and other psychotic disorders feature various psychopathological domains with distinctive courses, patterns of treatment-response, and prognostic implications as alluded by Tandon, (Tandon, R. 2013. p. 17. para. 6). The dimensional approach of DSM diagnosis has been discovered that it helps and chart the course of the disorder, which, distinguishes between normal and abnormal, thus can be used to screen for mental disorders, (Nussbaum. APA, 2013, p. 16). "It is increasingly evident that mental illness will be best understood as disorders of brain structure and function that implicate specific domains of cognition, emotion, and behavior." (Liebermann and Insel, 2013). The symptoms of mental illness can be very severe depending on the patients and the stages they are on their illnesses. Some symptoms include disorganized thought patterns, cognitive impairments, depression, anxiety disorders and catatonia. Therefore, it is imperative for clinical psychologists to follow set up criteria outlined in DSM for accurate diagnosis because the goal is to have accurate diagnosis and to have effective treatment for clients. Schizoaffective disorder is unstable diagnosis, and it usually leads to fully blown schizophrenia. If schizophrenia is not treated earlier than expected, with specific interventions, it leads to brain damage.

The question about psychosis-related symptoms whether they are indicative of schizophrenia diagnosis have been proven to be not the case. The psychosis symptoms do not indicate schizophrenia diagnosis. Tandon, reiterates the research conducted which proves that the psychosis-related symptoms do not always leads to schizophrenia diagnosis disorder. "Although individuals with a defined attenuated psychosis syndrome are five hundred-times more likely than the general population to develop a psychotic disorder in the next year (25), the vast majority of such individuals do not develop schizophrenia," (Tandon. R. 2013, p. 18. Para. 5). The DSM-5 treatment of schizophrenia including psychotic disorders are designed to facilitate clinical assessment and treatment to clients.

Psychotherapy

Transference in therapy is a situation whereby the feelings, desires, anxiety, and concepts from another person are redirected and applied to another person to enhance therapeutic setting. The emotions and feelings that the client experienced during his/her childhood or with their teachers, parents, relatives, or someone who had influence in his/her life, especially negatively, then those feelings are directed to the therapist. Sigmund Freud developed the concept of countertransference to refer to a situation in which the psychologist's emotions, unconsciously, are transferred influenced by a person in therapy and the reaction by the psychologist is called countertransference (Good-Therapy, 2007). www.goodtherapy.org). Kraemer alludes that his practical reasons to uphold countertransference as good and normal is that it exists because it is inevitable, according to many authors (Kraemer, W. P. p. 30. para. 2. 1958). According to Kraemer's assertion, countertransference becomes part of the therapist's blind spot, and it cannot be dismissed in terms of bias. Both Jung and Freud emphasize making and controlling conscious contents.

Freud continues to hold on saying that both ego and shadow are accepted as essential counter parts in psychic wholeness (Ibid. 30. para. 2). Servedio brings another concept about transference. He propounds that transference in terms of communication cannot be one-sided proposition but both transference and countertransference are universal phenomenon, which is relevant in analytical setting, (Servedio E. 1956. p. 392) quoted by (Kraemer, 1958, p. 32. para. 1). Social counsellors, physicians, surgeons, church ministers, the demands made on them are not usually seen as transference and countertransference which leads to anger, anxiety, guilt, uncertainty (Kraemer, 1958, p.32. para. 2). The transference and countertransference are seen as integral part of interpersonal psychotherapy in the way. Transference is an indispensable element of analytical work that plays fundamental role in interpersonal psychotherapy. The analyst must take sides with the instincts and struggle against ego and its resistances which resist repetition, hence, opposes transference of instinctual impulses, (Racker, H., 1970. p. 15. para. 2). Transference was, as resistance, but now it is considered the resisted, rejected, (Ibid. p.15. para. 2).

Transference and countertransference play important role in interpersonal psychotherapy approach as has proven to be effective to practice if the skills, techniques, and interventions are utilized and practiced properly. The Interpersonal therapy focuses on specific problem of the client and can reduce the symptoms and can create good relationships. To understand the client's unconscious impulses, resistance, and transference through intuition, makes the therapist to understand unresolved conflicts reflected in the client (Ibid. p. 16. para. 3). It can enhance problem solving and increase communication skills needed to anchor relationships. These promote interpersonal awareness and learning, resulting in improved relational capacity and symptom reduction. The social learning processes promote both intrapersonal and interpersonal change and enhances communication skills (Anchin, 1982. p. 117. Para. 2).

Interpersonal Psychology approach to practice presents both benefits as well challenges. The benefits for using interpersonal psychology approach are that it helps to identify problems expressed in emotions, learning skills to foster good rapport, and it focuses on specific problem areas that need to be addressed. It can assist to solve problems, conflicts, disputes thus improve the therapist's skills of communication by addressing issues such as depression, anxiety, and be able administer treatment and symptoms for social adjustment for clients.

The intuitive grasp is manifested through one's unconsciousness for self-assessment, (Racker, H. p. 17). Interpersonal psychotherapy comes with some challenges and limitations that the therapist should be aware of. When you are with the client in the process of therapy, the therapist must empathize with the client but sometimes the clients do not recognize one's empathy. Instead, they would attack you verbally. The therapist should be caring, non-judgmental, inspire hope, be able to repair ruptures and to find new ways that are better for the clients but sometimes the clients do not see the way out. The clients' conquering resistances and admitting the instinctual and emotional complexes which has the flashbacks from his past into his consciousness, impeded by unexpected phenomenon of the transference. Freud discovered that the analyst's work is like his, also that the impulses and feelings towards the client and Freud called this phenomenon countertransference (Racker, p.18. para. 2).

Somatic Symptoms and Related Disorder, Dissociative Disorder

The client in the case study has anxiety disorder according to DSM criteria and of course, somatic symptoms disorder. There is no medical evidence found for her chronic pain, according to the physicians. In that case, Factious Disorder can be assigned to her also which alludes to exaggerated symptoms depicting physical immobility. The client is restless, very anxious, in pain all over her body after the accident. She says that she has touch aches, feels nausea, does not go to work sometimes because she would be in pain all over her body. She lost her husband five years ago and she seems to be frustrated, depressed, and stressed with everything. This is typical symptoms of Somatic Symptoms and Related Disorder, Dissociated Disorders,

(Laureate Education. (Producer). (2012). 4 Minutes). To assign the client with DSS according to DSM criteria is because she shows extended stress and anxiety disorder American Psychiatric Association, 2013).

She has mental illness and the confounding factors that indicate mental disorder is her unrest, anxiety, distress, paranoia, and uncontrollable. These are symptoms of Somatic Symptoms Disorder (SSD) and Dissociative Disorder (DID) because her symptoms seem to be severe and as a result, it disrupts her life. It is Personality Disorder which the client constantly changes her behavior. She portrays unconscious defense mechanisms to protect from being judged by her behavior. Post Stress Traumatic Disorder (PST) can be assigned to the client as she was involved in an accident in which the health fraternity did not admit or diagnose with some injuries. She claims that since she had the accidents, she has stomach, chest pain and nausea.

It will be a challenge to assign medical treatment for the client since the physicians could not find anything wrong with the client, medically. She should be having emotional and psychological issues that need therapy. She says that she does not want to take any drugs for medication. That is the reason why she came for consultation instead of going to the hospital (Laureate Education, 2012; APA). The client may be diagnosed with multiple disorders, however, the Somatic Symptoms Disorder (SSD) is the major diagnosis when assigned DSM-criteria.

Cultural Competency Challenges

Cultural competency is one of the fundamental heartbeats of clinical professional psychology for which every practitioner should be aware of, confront it and learn to love it without which failure will be looming. As we now live in a global village, every practitioner will meet diverse patients/clients that he/she is not familiar with their cultures, customs, norms, religions, belief systems, ethics and of course, their educational backgrounds hence the importance of culturally competent. In fact, the society's diversity and the progressive development of individuals, families and societies will compel clinical professional psychologist to be more tolerant and patient with other cultures that they have never lived with or among. The challenges of cultural shock should be regarded as strengths and not as weaknesses. Ethnocultural groups that professional practitioners are working with need to be understood in their contexts. "The balance may be achieved elegantly using cultural adaptation procedures. We define cultural adaptation as the systematic modification of an evidence-based treatment (EBT) or intervention protocol to consider language, culture, and context in such a way that it is compatible with the client's cultural patterns, meanings, and values," Bernal, G., Jiménez-Chafey, M. I., & Domenech-Rodrígues, M. M. (2009). P. 261. "An evidence-based cultural adaptation has the potential to provide a methodology to modify treatments in a systematic manner so that the culture and context of diverse groups are considered," Ibid. p. 361.

Given that background, I find myself in a challenging position when working with a group of people I am not familiar with. However, I have worked with various and diverse groups of people which may reduce my ability to work with them, ethically and competently. My personal challenge will be working with the Asians Americans. Their culture and belief systems, their values, languages, do not match with African culture. The fact that they did not colonize Africa unlike the European imperialists, makes us disconnect with the Asians. Europeans and Westerners mingled with Africans during slavery, colonialism and thereafter when they imposed their cultures, values, and their thinking patterns. Africans can work better with the White people because of the historical backgrounds. After the end of slavery, the Whites and Blacks were forced to live together although they were some intensive racisms, and discrimination. The Union measures such as the Confiscation Acts and Emancipation Proclamation in 1863, the war ended slavery. The Thirteenth Amendment in December 1865 became a legal institution in USA. Wikipedia, (n.d.). Retrieved November 6, 2018, from https//en.m. Wikipedia.org/wiki/ Slavery in the United States.

Therefore, the two groups of people, Black people and Whites were forced to live together in harmony although it did not happen till this day. However, both groups recognize their differences, but they understand each other better. With the Asians and Blacks, they have never had such exposure. Therefore, the biases and attitude between the Blacks and the Asians is very huge. Asians tend to despise the Africans more than what the Whites do. They regard Africans as inferior to them and they love to align with the Whites more. That's why it is rare to see marriages between an African and an Asian.

The cultural competence will be a challenge to have the Asians as my clients/patients because of that background. Their values, cultures, attitudes, and biases and my values, culture, attitude, and biases will humper my ability to work ethically and competently in my professional practice. However, I will try to minimize the biases by being culturally respectful, loving, kind and developing good relationships with them. "The delivery of ethical and culturally consistent therapeutic approaches has continued to challenge practitioners today because of demographic changes throughout the country, professional man-dates, and the complex manner in which culture is understood and manifested therapeutically," Gallardo, M. E., Johnson, J., Parham, T. A., & Carter, J. A. (2009). p. 246. This will be one of my greatest challenges to foster cultural competence in my clinical professional practice in working with Asians. The applied psychology is still challenged in adequately translating our theories and discourse around multicultural issues into practice.

Cultural Awareness and the Diagnosis

As a psychotherapist, it is fundamental to be aware that the world has become a global village in which people from all walks of life, with their belief systems, religions, cultures, norms, traditions, and their sexual orientations will converge at your area of expertise, seeking therapy. The practitioner should take it as his/her responsibility to learn other cultures for the sake of clients. The practitioner should know and understand the boundaries in which he/she should operate from. The boundaries for the clinical practitioners include understanding and being aware of "beneficence, nonmaleficence, fidelity, responsibility, integrity, justice, respect for people's rights and dignity," (American Psychological Association. 2017), from other diverse cultures. The boundaries are important to the professional psychologist because the boundaries keep the practitioner to be aware and respect the culture, religion, and the rights of the clients/ patients.

The psychotherapist may benefit from knowing the cultures of the clients and their perceptions for psychological disorder and diagnosis. Ethical and multicultural competency is fundamental to a professional psychology practitioner because of the diversity and global village we live in and one has to be aware of other cultures, traditions, norms, religions. It does not mean that the practitioner has to know the client's cultures deeply but just to be aware of, to acknowledge and to tolerate other people's cultures is fundamental. Being respectful, developing good relationships, reading extensively about diverse cultures and religions, understanding people's ethical values in their own contexts, and promoting healthy eating, exercise, and education. "The balance may be achieved elegantly with cultural adaptation procedures. We define cultural adaptation as the systematic modification of an evidence-based treatment (EBT) or intervention protocol to consider language, culture, and context in such a way that it is compatible with the client's cultural patterns, meanings, and values," Bernal, G., Jiménez-Chafey, M. I., & Domenech-Rodrígues, M. M. (2009). P. 261.

The demographic changes of the country pose some challenges to professional psychology practitioner, but those challenges must be met head-on in order to bring about stability and professionalism in the field of psychology. "The delivery of ethical and culturally consistent therapeutic approaches has continued to challenge practitioners today because of demographic changes throughout the country, professional mandates, and the complex manner in which culture is understood and manifested therapeutically," Gallardo, M. E., Johnson, J., Parham, T. A., & Carter, J. A. (2009). p. 246.

The professional psychology practitioner ought to understand the matrix of cultures and ethical values of his/her patients/client as alluded by Bernal, Jimenez-Chafey, and Domenech-Rodrigues. When demography changes in the society, so does the field of psychology changes in order to meet those challenges. When the country changes demographically, with diverse cultures, and influx population, history teaches that even knowledge, skills, attitudes change to meet the challenges from one generation to another. Cross-cultural misunderstanding between the providers and the patients can create negative underpinnings that can have lasting impacts in the lives of any given group of people. Cultural perceptions of substance use may influence the client diagnosis. Some clients may be using certain drugs that are illegal in other states and other countries such as marijuana, as their medications for certain illnesses while other cultures may use certain drugs as their cultural practice as a tradition.

There is a smaller percentage indicating that the adolescents who develop some problems with substance abuse may affect their development in the future (Burrow-Sanchez, J. J. 2006. p. 283. Para. 1 &). The drug laws influential context poses risk factors and substance availability to the adolescent. The protective factors dramatically decrease the probability of the individuals to use drugs and it is important for the therapist to discuss preventative measures with the clients even if the cultures permit the use of drugs. Each state has developed the criteria for drug use, and it is upon the therapists to use the criterion used by each state to limit or permit drug use for medical purposes. The relevance of cultural and health disparities into today's psychotherapy is fundamental. "This has led to positive developments such as the requirement that 'cultural competence standards' (ensuring practitioner's awareness on such issues as culturally related attitudes, symptoms, language and interpretation of clinical data) be developed in state systems in efforts to improve access and quality of care." (Escobar, J. I., & Vega, W. A. (2006, p. 42. Para. 7.)

Professional psychology has started to shift toward a competent-based model training in recent decades. There has been some significance made towards competencies in professional psychology. Donovan, R. A. and Ponce, A. N., (2009). The shift to the culture of competence-based model ushers a new dimension into addressing public trust and protection to the citizen. Donovan and Ponce assert, "Other potential benefits include: a more flexible training model based on the trainees' needs and progress toward established goals... improved connections between graduate training and the skills needed to practice as a psychologist, anticipating likely increased competency requirements by federal and state regulatory bodies... and keeping pace with other health care professions ..." Donovan, R. A., and Ponce, A. N., (2009). p. 546. This new shift brings with it new and high anticipation and zeal to the psychology fraternity. The evolution to change the old model and the contribution and benefits of the competence-based education will forever change the perspective and the paradigm of thinking. Donovan and Ponce reiterate the fact that, "the foundational competencies address the 'knowledge, skills, attitudes, and values' psychologists need in their professional roles... and the functional competencies address the functions psychologists perform," (para. 2), to add value and create relationships between the clinical psychologists and the patients.

The competency-based education movement for the training of professional psychologists contributes a benchmark in the professional psychology in that it outlines the core foundational and functional competencies in three levels of professional development i.e., readiness practicum, internship, and entry to practice, (Fouad, Nadya. A., Grus, Catharine. L., Hatcher, Robert. L., Kaslow Nadine. J., Hutchings, P. S., Madison, M. B. Crossman, R. E., e'al, 2009). 55. The licensing board have documented the requirements of acquired evidence of competence in all levels in training the professional psychology. The competencies include habitual and judicious use of communication, knowledge, technical skills, clinical reasoning, emotions, values, and reflection in daily practice, to benefit individuals and the community. The competencies include knowledge, skills and attitudes that are required to bring about the change necessary to modernize the new model, Fouad, Nadya. A., Grus, Catharine. L., Hatcher, Robert. L., Kaslow Nadine. J., Hutchings, P. S., Madson, M. B. Crossman, R. E. e'al, 2009). Para. 2. Cube model is one of the core competency areas in psychology which has been accepted and has gained recognition in the training of clinical psychology students.

The role and the importance of the relationship competency to the practice of professional psychology is by design, aimed at developing relationship with the client in order to gain trust and mutual understanding between the clinician and the patients. "The path broadens through the development of trust, safety, and understanding as the relationship develops," Capuzzi, D., and Stauffer D. M., (2016). The relationship competency to the professional psychology has gained popularity in recent decades and Kaslow points out the eight elements: "Eight of the 10 workgroups were formed around competency domains: (a) ethical and legal issues, (b) individual and cultural diversity, (c) scientific foundations and research, (d) psychological assessment, (e) intervention, (f) consultation and interprofessional collaboration, (g) supervision, and (h) professional development," Kaslow, Nadine J. (2004). To develop relationships with your clients/patients, the clinician must develop and foster good rapport with them. The relationship competency for professional psychology demands that nowadays. Understanding cultural diversity and cultural values, religions, and ethical and legal issues of an organization one works with cultivates and develops relationships. This includes the relationship with the staff one works with, the boards, the management, and the institution.

Destructive Trends in Mental Health: The Well-Intentioned Path to Harm

By Rogers H. Wright and Nicholas A. Cummings

In the 21st-century modern era, according to Cummings and O'Donoghue, most people are taking "soma" to alleviate anxieties and bipolar depression. "As unlikely as this seemed in the 1930s, many authorities are now sounding the alarm that our current society is overmedicating itself rather than addressing and solving everyday problems, thus rendering itself and future generations less and less able to face the normal exigencies of living…"[59] They continue to elude that what is more disturbing is that the pharmaceutical is making a lot of money on the expense of the populace. More disturbing is that there is a trend they prescribe psychotropic medications to adolescents, children, and even preschoolers which compromises child development.

The political correctness that permits the pharmaceutical industry to play the tunes according to the political parties which are in power has spawned so much harm to the populace because of the drug pandemic. The discussion of political correctness in correcting the mindset of valuing money over humans is a disaster and catastrophic as political correctness is invading mental health which detects the treatment of mental health.

The book critically, evaluates the fundamental issue of cultural sensitivity towards restoring cultural values, lack of clarity, about the implication for ethical behaviors. William discusses the effects of the negative things compounded by a lack of cultural sensitivity. The book also evaluates the construct of cultural competence with diverse disciplines and domains. It invites practical objectives with scientifically grounded evidence. It criticizes the cultural competence construct and the evaluation of applied psychology. William contrasts the disciplines within clinical, school, and counseling in psychology. His discussion on cultural sensitivity stimulates dialogue and debate among professionals across the field of academia.

"Being culturally sensitive is not simply associated with conjecture on what practices will result in the best progress in psychology; it also has become ethically controlled" (cited in Sue et al., 1999, p. 533). It has been assumed that psychologists from the same ethnic groups may reduce underutilization is yet to be proven. It is, known that the same kind of people treat each other honorable and with dignity, which is the concept of homogeneous unit principle.

"Hierarchy, inequality, and violence have historically been part of human social structures. There have always been rulers and ruled, leaders and followers, the fortunate and the needy, and the powerful and the weak. Various cultures have treated disparities in status, power, fortune, and ability in different ways." In many countries, the victims are blamed for their behaviors, for example, if the woman is raped, she is blamed for her attire which might have attracted men or her reckless behavior that she was loose. On the other hand, men are blamed for perpetuating violence as they are stronger than women and because of their masculinity, they are blamed for forcing women to comply with their demands.

Victim blaming is common. Sin influences people to do things contrary to social and ethical normal. Instead of shifting blame, it is imperative to increase the understanding of the dynamics and the origins of victimhood. The whole concept is not to blame the victim instead investigate the causes, the intent and find solutions to deal with the problem. In a Christian context, sin is

---

[59] Rogers H. Wright and Nicholas A. Cummings, *Destructive Trends in Mental Health: The Well-Intentioned Path to Harm,* (New York: Taylor and Francis Groups), 2005, 3.

the root of all evil, and Christ is the answer to every problem. Seeking God's Word and what it says about sin and what it says about Christ is the best solution.

"There is an overdiagnosis of ADD/ADHD, or these conditions are far more amenable to behavioral interventions than heretofore has been acknowledged. They question the cerebral malfunctioning theory as it is applied to the currently inflated and criteria-diluted population of patients and suggest that social forces are..."[60] It is really, puzzling to learn that "organized psychiatry has remained silent regarding the overuse of medication with children and adolescents, understandably, when one realizes that medication and hospitalization have remained that professional.

Psychologists, psychiatrists, pharmacology all work together without considering much about the health of people, especially children for that matter. What is even more complicated is the psychophysiological state that can co-exist in the same personality, called (alters). There are differences in the brain waves activity. The kinds of disorders confuse the minds of the scientists, psychologists, physicians but they don't want to acknowledge all these complications of the symptoms or diagnosis.

Conclusion

The chapter captures the essence of what clinical psychology has affected human health. The chapter addresses substance use, and effects to adolescents. Transference and counter transference are explored in the chapter and personal disorder. The medical condition, the use of hypnosis in therapy and the impacts of clinical psychology opens up the pandora box that need to be discussed in depth and find the solution. Somatic symptoms, cultural awareness and competency are some of the subjects discussed in the chapter. The chapter concludes with the therapies available such as psychodynamic/object relation therapy, behavioral therapy, cognitive therapy, cognitive behavioral therapy, clinic enclective therapy, Gottman/marriage therapy, EMDR therapy, social skills training therapy, dialectical behavioral therapy and the group therapy.

---

[60] Ibid.

CHAPTER THREE

Biblical Context of Human Health

Biblical Health of Body and Mind

It is imperative to look at and discuss the biblical health for the human body in contrast to both clinical and anthropological perspective of human body. Based on biblical texts and the narration of human body, according to God's instructions about food. Let us examine together the original instructions that gave to the first man and the first woman in the garden of Eden, in Genesis. The body and the mind play pivotal roles in the function of the body, and they are to be nurtured, cared, and be protected. The mind includes the emotions, intellect, and the faculty of consciousness.

God gave human beings the food to eat just like He gave the animals. "If you diligently heed the voice of the Lord your God and do what is right in His sight, give ear to His commandments and keep all His statutes, I will put none of the diseases on you which I have brought on the Egyptians. For I am the Lord who heals you," (Exodus 15:26, KJV). "For I will restore health to you and heal you of your wounds…," (Jeremiah 30:17, KJV). God has given people food to eat (He upholds the cause of the oppressed and gives food to the hungry, (Psalm 146:7, JKV). The LORD sets prisoners free. Every living creature will be food for you; as I gave the green plants, I have given you everything. God said, "I have given you every plant with seeds on the face of the earth and every tree that has fruit with seeds. This will be your food," (Genesis 1:29, KJV). "And to all the beasts of the earth and all the birds in the sky and all the creatures that move along the ground–everything that has the breath of life in it–I give every green plant for food," (Genesis 1:30, KJV). "The eyes of all, look to you, and you give them their food at the proper time. He gives food to every creature. His love endures forever," (Psalm 136:25, KJV). What affect the mind, body and emotions is mostly the food one eats.

Lane and Tripp put their efforts together to write book pregnant with Biblical discourse in teaching and training those who desire to learn and to teach others to connect them with their creator. Lane and Tripp challenge believers to understand what they ought to do at the right and for the right purpose. They quote (II Peter 1:3-9, NIV) in which Peter discusses the missing gap. First, Peter starts with God's word saying that his divine power has given us everything we need for life and godliness through our knowledge of him, his promises to escape the corruption in the world caused by evil desires. However, to escape such challenges in life, God has granted us faith goodness, knowledge, self-control, perseverance, godliness, kindness, and love. They discuss the reasons the believers fail to produce the fruit of faith. Their lives are not characterized by peaceful, loving, and balanced relationships. They highlight that these believers leave a trail of broken relationships, a struggle with material things, and a lack of personal growth. Paul mentions the kind of believers they are, "who have the form of godliness but denying its power" (I Timothy 3:5, NIV).

The counterfeit hopes are false hopes, and the Bible is very clear about false hopes that are deceitful and their bondage. Lane and Tripp discuss the alternative theories which give false hope. Christ is to fill the gap in our lives and that gap is the gospel gap. In their book, they point out things that fill the gap, such as formalism, legalism, mysticism, activism, biblicism, psychologism, socialism, etc. and these are plausible lies, according to the Bible.

Biblical Health for the Soul/Spirit

William Glasse outlines facts about his experience as a psychiatrist for forty-fives in the practice. He alludes that all the people that were referred to him were all unhappy people regardless of their symptoms. They were unhappy and things did not go according to their wishes. He indicates that clients were not mentally ill. They had no pathology in their brains. He says that mental illness should not be applied to them. William categorically says people who should be referred to with pathology in the brain are those people who suffer from Parkinson's or Alzheimer's diseases. He says that the only way to help people who claim to be mentally ill is to counsel them. That's when Biblical Counseling can be applied, not any other kind of counseling.

William gives his suggestion that those people who are unhappy can be taught to improve their mental health through Choice Theory, a new form of Psychology that he created to improve their relationships. All human efforts and solutions to help mental health cannot bring solutions except if people can be referred to the Scripture that gives and guides any individual to find peace and joy, which supersedes human understanding.

He continues to say that the whole invasion of child ADHD in childhood and adolescence is accompanied by a concurrent explosion of such diagnoses into adulthood... "It should be understood that hyperactivity and distractibility, although present, are less dramatic symptoms that are understandable and of less concern to the patient." Some of these terms that the psychologists and the psychiatrists tag are of no use but to advance their agendas to masquerade money at the expense of innocent people. These are the side effects of the high activities of human life. The anxiety, depression, and distress of life are going to be there, but God designed it that way and if we come to Him in sincerity, He counsels us through the Holy Spirit.

Scott O. Lilienfeld and others propound, "Pseudoscientific and unscientific claims hold an understandable allure for the practitioners and the public. Many fringe therapeutic techniques promise quick fix or overnight cure for longstanding psychological conditions." Several of the pseudo-scientific promises are rapid and simplistic solutions to complex life problems but in fact, they damage the health of many people.

The therapeutic techniques that are being applied damage the brains and neuro-systems and when they are damaged, they are irreversible. There is increasing substantial evidence that some of the psychological treatments are harmful. There is evidence that some communities are now moving and addressing threats posed by unsubstantiated psychotherapies. Soul-care through Biblical Counseling is the only solution when the Biblical Counselor uses the Scripture. God has the way to restore people's health through His sovereign means.

"This contention that dysfunctional behavior is inherited is unproven. No good scientific evidence supports it… The assumption that ADHD symptoms arise from cerebral multifunctional has not been supported even after extensive investigation, and no consistent structural, functional, or chemical neurological marker is found in children with ADHD diagnosis as currently formulated." This scientific research proves that there is no evidence dysfunctional behaviors are inherited but these diseases are assigned and tagged by the psychologists and psychiatrists to take advantage of families as they cannot let their children suffer and die.

In 1969, the APA identified the freedom of reproductive choice as a mental health and child welfare issue. In the same vein, current research indicates that the existing medical controls and safety measures have not prevented chronic brain damage in boxers who have fought in recent years. On the political front, "APA opposes the use of corporal punishment in schools, juvenile facilities, childcare nurseries, and all other institutions, public and private where children are cared for or educated…" Social justice plays a critical role in defining community psychology. "Community psychology advocates another important value, respect for diversity, yet it does not practice this when it comes to socio political ideas."

"APA's ethical principles urge psychologists to be sensitive to cultural differences. However, despite these ideals, the lack of sociopolitical diversity continues… This lack of political diversity has unintended negative consequences and is detrimental to psychology in ways that conflict with the profession's core values and ethical principles." Psychologists should engage in advocacy when there is strong empirical evidence bearing on the social policy in question.

Complete Human Health Trichotomy

The complete human health trichotomy completes the anatomy of a human being composed of body, soul, and spirit. For the human body to function normally, and well-balanced, the three should coordinate in an efficient and in congruent. They are many theories about the human anatomy. Some believe that a human being is composed of Body, Soul, and Spirit, the trichotomists, while the dichotomists argue that a human being is composed of the Body and the Soul.

The argument at stake is to distinguish the differences between the body, soul, and spirit in humanity. "The Bible teaches that humanity possesses a physical body, a soul, and a spirit. Regarding how these aspects of the human nature connect with and relate to each other, there are four primary theories. Two of the views, anthropological monism and anthropological hylomorphism, deal primarily with how the three aspects of humanity combine to form the human nature. The two other models, dichotomy (anthropological dualism) and trichotomy, deal with the distinction between the human soul and human spirit. The distinction between the material (physical) and immaterial (spiritual) aspects of the human nature is straightforward."[61] The Bible has certain verses that allude and use the soul and the spirit interchangeably, (Matthew 10:28, NKJV; Luke 1:46-47, NKJV; and I Corinthians 5:3; 7:34, NKJV). "Those who believe that human nature is a trichotomy typically believe the following: the physical body is what connects us with the physical world around us, the soul is the essence of our being, and the spirit is what connects us with God…, Those who believe that human nature is a dichotomy would have the same understanding of the body but would view the spirit as the part of the soul that connects with God."[62] These are Christian and Biblical views.

The debates between trichotomy and dichotomy schools of thoughts can go on and on without logical conclusion but can be left as a hypothesis. "People who believe in trichotomy believe that the physical body connects human beings to the world. They also believe that the spirit is part of the soul that connects human beings with God… While dichotomy vs. trichotomy tries to identify whether the spirit and soul are different aspects of human nature, both theories remain Biblically plausible."[63] The body, the material is a vehicle in which the soul and the spirit are contained but they are eternal. The immaterial, the soul and the spirit are invisible and untouchable. They make the body function well and to be well-balanced. Soul in Greek is *Psychi* and Psychology is the study of soul. It means the soul (*psychi*) cannot be treated by any medication or any that is material. The analogy in this context is that the soul can be

---

[61] https://www.gotquestions.org/trichotomy-dichotomy.html, (Accessed, November 1, 2022).

[62] Ibid.

[63] http://www.differencebetween.net/miscellaneous/religion-miscellaneous/difference-between-dichotomy-and-trichotomy/, (Accessed November 1, 2022).

treated by means of spirit, (*pneuma*), breathe or blow, the breath of life hence Biblical Counseling is Biblically based, and Christ centered. The Holy Spirit (*pneuma*) has, therefore, the power to connect the soul to its creator, who is the source of life. In Hebrew, the word spirit, (*Ruach*), and in Greek (*Pneuma*), refer to invisible, unchangeable, immaterial spirit or soul that do not belong to material world. Paul expounds, "Christ is the visible image of the invisible God…." (Colossians 1:15-17).

Conclusion

Human Health is fundamental as the body and the mind were explored in this chapter to come into terms with the Biblical health of the body and the mind. The mind includes the emotions, intellect, and the faculty of consciousness. The body, the soul and the spirit are pivotal in human function and coordination. The destructive trends in mental health and its impact in human health have left humanity in confusion and awe. The dichotomy and trichotomy views or beliefs were explored in the chapter, and it remained as hypothesis that does not have a definitive answer to their thrust.

CHAPTER FOUR

Medical & Biblical Contrast

Medical VS Biblical Approach toward Human Health

This chapter captures the essence of the medical approach toward human health versus the Biblical approach toward human health. In this discussion, medical approach will be examined in physical perspective and then Biblical approach will be reviewed in spiritual perspective. Medical treatment is focused on the physical and biological abnormalities to make normal in the human body. Medication, therefore, cannot heal the broken spirit or soul but the physical only, with flesh and blood. *Psychi* (Greek), soul, cannot be treated by medication which is substance or matter because the spiritual entity cannot be treated the physical. There is no synergy between spiritual and the physical. Physical or biological entity is treated with matter or substance which is physical. Spiritual matters are treated with spiritual phenomenon. Breggin describes the current mental health providers prescribing psychotropic drugs as "medication spellbinding. "All psychotropics drugs are neurotoxins that are designed to attack the brain and cause it to not function the way it was designed to function. The brain fights back because it wants to function the way it is designed to function. This is why prescribers must experiment with dosages and try alternative medications to get the desired effects."[64] Trying to treat a spiritual problem with a substance or a pill does not address the spiritual problem.

"The following symptoms, anxiety, agitation, panic attacks, insomnia, irritability, hostility, aggressiveness, impulsivity, akathisia (psychomotor restlessness), hypomania, and mania, have been reported in adult and pediatric patients being treated with antidepressants for major depressive disorder as well as for other indications, both psychiatric and nonpsychiatric."[65]

---

[64] Breggin, Peter; Cohen, David. Your Drug May Be Your Problem: How to Stop Taking Psychiatric Medications. (Philadelphia: Da Capo Books, 2007), 10.
[65] Ibid.

Psychotropic/Psychoactive drugs have very real, adverse effects for those taking them, both short- and long-term.

Robert Whitaker explains, one basic premise of this work is that the disproved "chemical imbalance" theory has led to the development of medications that try to fix a problem that doesn't exist, and thereby alter brain chemistry and worsen symptoms of various mental illnesses. Soul (*psych*) is not the physical brain, but beyond the physical. When the human brain adjusts to these changes, it changes the way the cells of the brain signal one another and the way genes are expressed. A person's brain begins to function in a way that is "qualitatively as well as quantitatively different from the normal state."[66]

We are body, we are mind, we are spirit as created in the image of God, (*Imago Dei*). We are these things. What impacts one aspect of our being impacts the other aspects of our being. A biblical, anthropology, and a historical Christian perspective on the *Imago Dei* of humanity, affirm the spirituality, the physical and the emotional being of a person.

Psychology VS Biblical Solutions to Human Health

William Glasse outlines facts about his experience as a psychiatrist for forty-fives in the practice. He alludes that all the people that were referred to him were all unhappy people regardless of their symptoms. They were unhappy and things did not go according to their wishes. He indicates that clients were not mentally ill and that they had no pathology in their brains. He says that the mental illness should not be applied to them. William categorically says people who should be referred to with pathology in the brain are those people who suffer from Parkinson's or Alzheimer's diseases. He says that the only way to help people who claim to be mentally ill is to counsel them. That's when Biblical Counseling can be applied, not any other kinds of counseling or therapies.

William gives his suggestion that those people who are unhappy can be taught to improve their mental health through Choice Theory, a new form of Psychology that he created to improve their relationships. All human efforts and solutions to help mental health cannot bring solutions except if people can be referred to the Scripture that gives and guides any individual to find peace and joy, which supersedes human understanding. Biblical Counseling ushers the original and authentic solutions to human health because it taps the fundamental source of human problem and human solution, pointing to the Scriptures and Christ who is the source of life. This psychological pandemic has, in recent years, leaped to children.

"Every parent has noticed, particularly with younger children, that toward the end of an especially exciting and fatiguing day children are literally 'ricocheting off the walls.'

---

[66] Ibid.

Although this behavior may in the broadest sense be classifiable as hyperactivity, it is generally pathognomonic of nothing more than excessive fatigue, for which the treatment of choice is a good night's sleep."[67]

He continues to say that the whole invasion of child ADHD in childhood and adolescence is accompanied by a concurrent explosion of such diagnoses into adulthood... "It should be understood that hyperactivity and distractibility, although present, are less dramatic symptoms that are understandable and of less concern to the patient."[68] Some of these terms that the psychologists and the psychiatrists tag are of no use but to advance their agendas to masquerade money at the expense of innocent people. These are the side effects of the high activities of human life. The anxiety, depression, and distress of life are going to be there but God designed it that way and if we come to Him in sincerity, He counsels us through the Holy Spirit.

Scott O. Lilienfeld and others propound, "Pseudoscientific and unscientific claims hold an understandable allure for the practitioners and the public. Many fringe therapeutic techniques promise quick fix or overnight cure for longstanding psychological conditions."[69] A few pseudo-scientific promises are rapid and simplistic solutions to complex life problems but in fact, they damage the health of many people.

The therapeutic techniques that are being applied damage the brains and neural systems and when they are damaged, they are irreversible. There is increasing substantial evidence that some of the psychological treatments are harmful. There is evidence that some communities are now moving and addressing threats posed by unsubstantiated psychotherapies.

Soul-care through Biblical Counseling is the only solution when the Biblical Counselor uses the Scripture. God has the way to restore people's health through His sovereign means. "This contention that dysfunctional behavior is inherited is unproven. No good scientific evidence supports it... The assumption that ADHD symptoms arise from cerebral multifunctional has not been supported even after extensive investigation, and no consistent structural, functional, or chemical neurological marker is found in children with ADHD diagnosis as currently formulated."[70] These scientific researches prove that there is no evidence dysfunctional behaviors are inherited but these diseases are assigned and tagged by the psychologists and psychiatrists to take advantage of families as they cannot let their children suffer and die.

The Bible is the Word of God which is the final authority in every situation or circumstances in life and it has the answer to any human problem. "For the word of God is living and powerful, and sharper than any two-edged sword, piercing even to the division of soul and spirit, and of joints and marrow, and is a discerner of the thoughts and intents of heart," (Hebrews 4:12),

---

[67] Ibid. 130.
[68] Ibid. 135.
[69] Ibid. 195.
[70] Ibid. 219.

NKJV. "All Scripture is given by inspiration of God, and is profitable for doctrine, for reproof, for correction, for instruction, for instruction in righteousness, that the man of God may be complete, thoroughly equipped for every good work," (II Timothy 3:16-17, NKJV). "Authority, the Reformed contended that all things must be tested 'by Scriptures alone' (sola Scriptura),"[71]

God the Father in the Godhead's function was the creation of the world and sustaining it in His bosom. God the Father is the life giver, with authority and power. He is omniscient, omnipotent, and omnipresent with infinite power. He is the healer, merciful, forgives and loves. He is the source of life, the sender, and the planner of salvation to all those who believe in him. God is the source of life revealed through Jesus (John 6:30-40, NKJV); John 1:4-14, NKJV). Both Biblical counselors and counselees must submit to the authority of Christ.

Medical Anthropology - Biomedical

The biomedical stems from the biocultural aspects that shape certain populations that respond to modern medical interventions. It considers human biology and health, necessitates the skeletal, the molecular and the population of certain group of people and particular disease. The major research in biomedical include neuroscience, cancer biology, regenerative medicine, and reproductive biology. Biomedicine contends that illness is caused by deviations from universal biological norms into biological abnormality. "As the world becomes increasingly multicultural and mobile, combining cultural understanding with biomedical knowledge is growing in importance. Because of this, biomedical anthropology focuses not only on molecular or cellar mechanism of pathology and the transmission and the dissemination of diseases but also bio sociocultural factors that affect health outcomes for both individual and the populations,"[72] Biomedical anthropology enhances the understanding of anthropology, human health, illness, and human biology, including sociocultural and cross-cultural perspective. It examines culture, race, ethnicity, class, gender, and inequality and emphasizes effective cross-cultural communication which is vital in human ethnography.

Medical Anthropology - Sociomedical

Sociomedical covers evolutionary medicine, species ethnography, disease ecology, examining human disease, health, medicine, and human ecology. All this to address human health to restore their humanity and dignity not to succumb to catastrophic human demise. The field addresses

---

[71] Joel R. Beeke, *Living for God's Glory*: An Introduction to Calvinism, (Orland: Reformation Trust), 2008, p. 133.
[72] https://www.petersons.com/blog/biomedical-anthropology-a-degree-for-the-future-of-medicine-and-science/, by Ben, (November 29, 2017).

the social, historical, cultural, psychological, and economic realms on human health to advance social justice and to improve human health. Sociomedical aims to enhance public health and to explore sexuality, urban health, aging, homelessness, drug use and mental health and health care access to all. Sociomedical is connected to Social Sciences addressing historical, social, cultural, economic, psychological, and archeological issues that influence and affect human outcomes. Sociomedical can develop strategies that can help to make research on education, address health inequality, social justice, and other human social services. Social Sciences include education, housing, poverty, transport, health care organizations and environment that affect the population. Some of these factors enables and prevent loss of lives in the society.

Some of the major focuses of social medicine are as outlined by the medical anthropology of the causes, the spread, the treatment, and the prevention of diseases and illnesses.

Medical Anthropology – Epidemiology

Public Health's thrust is to protect the communities where they live, play, learn, work, and thrive. Basically, Epidemiology is the study of human health issues, and it deals with the incidents, control of diseases, distributing and health incentives and services to communities. Human diseases and disorder which spread along the frameworks of cultural and social structures hence the need of Epidemiology techniques to curb diseases. Epidemiology is fundamental in shaping human and public health to prevent catastrophic healthcare disaster.

Epidemiology enhances the fundamentals to develop clinical methodologies and research to improve health care systems. "Major areas of epidemiological study include disease causation, transmission, outbreak investigation, disease surveillance, environmental epidemiology, forensic epidemiology, occupational epidemiology, screening, biomonitoring, and comparisons of treatment effects such as in clinical trials. Epidemiologists rely on other scientific disciplines like biology to better understand disease processes, statistics to make efficient use of the data and draw appropriate conclusions, social sciences to better understand proximate and distal causes, and engineering for exposure assessment,"[73] Epidemiology plays a pivotal role in healthcare systems for research and to the particular group of people's understanding of their health, culture, diseases, treatment and prevention.

Every society or community needs Epidemiology research to curb the human diseases and the prevention to survive. "Epidemiological studies are aimed, where possible, at revealing unbiased relationships between exposures such as alcohol or smoking, biological agents, stress,

---

[73] https://en.wikipedia.org/w/index.php?search=&title=Special:Search, (Accessed February 10, 2023).

or chemicals to mortality or morbidity. The identification of causal relationships between these exposures and outcomes is an important aspect of epidemiology,"[74]

Conclusion

The chapter captured the essence of Medical Anthropology on how it relates to Medical versus Biblical approach on human health. The discussion on Biomedical, Sociomedical and Epidemiology was explored to determine how the human healthcare systems are affected by diseases surrounding the population in the world and to find ways to improve human health.

---

[74] Ibid.

CHAPTER FIVE

Medical Anthropology – Archeology & Biocultural

Archeology is a pivotal anchor in the understanding medical anthropology about human society and people's lives. Archelogy is a glue entity that puts puzzle pieces together of human life as scientific trajectory and ethos that governs humankind. It must be understood that "Archaeology is the systematic study of the human past through material remains. Archaeologists examine diverse remnants of human actions through excavation, recovery, and material analyses. Cultural systems through time and space are reconstructed by examining ancient social, political, religious, and economic systems through both a regional and comparative perspective. As such, archaeologists rely on a plethora of methods and techniques avenues including specific artifact analyses (bones, ceramics, lithics, paleobotany) as well as geographic information systems (GIS)."[75] In the same vein, archeology is coined together with biological anthropology to argument the accurate results of tests and evaluation the data gathered, using all kinds of reliable tools and instruments such as 14 carbon dating and other scientific instruments available.

As such, "Biological anthropology is the study of humans and non-human primates from an evolutionary and biocultural perspective. It is the most humanistic of scientific disciplines due to the complex cultural organization, institutions, and symbolism associated with human populations, yet the most biologically oriented humanistic discipline due to the unifying emphasis on evolutionary theory. Biological anthropologists' study diverse subject matter including the behavior and biology of non-human primates, the evolution of human populations based on fossil and genetic data, and the health, well-being, and resiliency of contemporary populations."[76] To complement biological archeology, there is also bioarcheology which focuses on the studies of skeletal remains. It entails that both biological anthropology and bioarcheology are taping their guidance from cultural anthropology and evolution biology. By the same token, the biocultural study zero ins on the interaction between biological and cultural phenomena

---

[75] https://soan.gmu.edu/about-overview/anthropology/archaeology, (Accessed March 6, 2023).
[76] Ibid.

which is foundational in informing the research institutions about the past remains of humans and animals skeletal in order to learn from the past societal way of life. If a group of people or a society forgets its past, it is ultimately, denying its destiny and renouncing or denouncing its future.

Archeology Theory and Methods

The archeology theory and methods used in the bioarcheology, cultural archeology and medical anthropology are meant to determine the past lifestyles, culture, food, tools, and other things used in the past to inform modern archeology. "Bioarcheologists use the methods of skeletal biology, mortuary archaeology, and the archaeological record to answer questions about the lives and lifestyles of past, Populations."[77] The archeological theory is the interaction and the different intellectual frameworks in which archeologists interpret archeological data and analyze them for scholarly research. They are three types of archeology, "Medieval archeology is the study of post-Roman European archaeology until the sixteenth century. Post-medieval archaeology is the study of material culture in Europe from the 16th century onwards. Modern archaeology is the study of modern society using archaeological methods …"[78] In the field of archeology, they are methods employed to gather data. "Archeologists use several methods to establish relative chronology including geologic dating, stratigraphy, seriation, cross-dating, and horizon markers… Geologic dating. Geologists study the earth and the natural forces that are involved in changes that take place."[79] All this is done to determine the age and the dates of the remains left behind.

Biocultural Impact on Human Health

The biocultural impact on human health goes beyond and above human imagination. Biocultural is research on human biology, culture, lifestyle, and medical ecology that is composed of social, cultural, and behavioral variables in the research designs aimed at finding accurate data about past. "Valuable models for studying the interface between biological and cultural factors affecting human well-being. Two models of biocultural research predominate in health studies: one which integrates biological, environmental, and cultural data, and a second, more segmented model in which biological data are primary and data on culture and environment

---

[77] Ibid.

[78] https://soan.gmu.edu/about-overview/anthropology/archaeology, (Accessed March 7, 2023).

[79] https://www.google.com/search?q=archaeological+method+and+theory, (Accessed March 7, 2023).

are secondary."[80] The biocultural impact on human health has a tremendous effect and it needs to be learned, preserved, and understood in the contextual of human spirit, dignity, and mutual respect.

It is imperative and fundamental to understand that history, culture, and humanity has been put in this planet for a purpose and has to be understood in both religious, spiritual and cultural perspective. "A biocultural approach provides an emerging framework for clarifying the mechanisms that connect water security to human health and wellbeing. Five basic tenets of the biocultural approach are outlined: The focus on the local, the centrality of culture, the notion of embodied disadvantage, a concern with proximate mechanisms to test theorized pathways…"[81]

Government and Civil Society Impact on Human Health

The government has been given authority to be a custodian of citizen in any given country, (Romans 13:1-2, NKJV). Although the governments are secular in nature and by design, they are mostly, governed by politicians who govern through civil governance, God enthrones and dethrones kings, (Daniel 2:21). The three offices of the government are: **Legislative** - Makes Laws (Congress, comprised of the House of Representatives and Senate). **Executive** - Carries out laws (President, Vice President, Cabinet). **Judicial** – Evaluates Laws (Supreme Court and other courts).

Health is human right and in the same vein, health care is right because every human being deserves to enjoy health care as the fundamental right and must be maintained and protected. Human health in drives the nation's economy, industry, commerce, tourism, and human resources. Unhealth nation is doomed to destruction because it does not have any potential, hope and a future. Quality medical care is responsible life expectancy in the nation. Many factors can improve life expectancy, including education, nutrition, hospitals, and health care systems. Human services, social goods and health care systems are the determinants of how the government impact human health in the country.

The environmental degradation, air-pollution, food insecurity, poor education systems, poor nutrition, poor transportation, and inadequate housing facilities can derail any country on its economic development. Community development and health care systems are engineered, propelled, and maintained by government entities and anchored by the local government branches.

---

[80] Ann McElroy, Medical Anthropology Quarterly, *International Journal for the Analysis of Health*, September 1990, https://anthrosource.onlinelibrary.wiley.com/, (Accessed March 7, 2023).

[81] Alexander A. Brewis, et al, WIREsWATER, **https://doi.org/10.1002/wat2.1440**, April 15, 2020, (Accessed March 7, 2023).

God and Nations

People struggling with fear concerning world events, there is good news that God's sovereignty covers the entire globe, and He watches the world events, and He is in control of everything. He sent Son, Jesus Christ to redeem the people from their sins and to redeem the world because everything belongs to Him. First, "For God has not given us the spirit of fear, but of power; and of love, and soul mind," (II Timothy 1:7, NKJV). "There is no fear in love; but perfect love casts out fear, because fear hath torment. He who fears is not made perfect in love," (I John 4:18, NKJV). If a counselee is consumed with fear of the world events, it is important who he/she is in Christ. The counselee has to be reminded that God is in control of everything. "God changes times and seasons; he deposes kings, and raises up others. He gives wisdom to the wise and knowledge to the discerning," (Daniel 2:21, NIV).

I would assign him/her Scriptures to read and to come out with his/her findings in the following session and share what he/she would have discovered, such as (Daniel 2:21; I John 4:18; II Tim. 1:7, NIV). "The decision is announced by messengers, the holy ones declare the verdict, so that the living may know that the highest is sovereign over all kingdoms on earth and gives them to anyone he wishes and sets over them the lowliest of people," (Daniel 4:17,NIV). The love of God has been poured into us through the Holy Spirit. God's love is perfect, unconditional, faithful, forgiving, pure, everlasting, and encompassing. God's love is revealed in Christ Jesus. God's love is *agape* (Greek), the love which is sacrificial and unconditional. "Give thanks to the God of heaven, for his steadfast love endures forever," (Psalm 136:26, ESV). "Dear friends, let us love one another, for love comes from God. Everyone who loves has been born of God and knows God. Whoever does not love does not know God, because God is love," (I John 4:7-8, NIV). "For God so loved the world that He gave His only begotten Son, that whoever believes in Him should not perish but have everlasting life," (John 3:16, NKJV). God loved, and He demonstrated His love by giving His only Son. "We love Him because He first loved us," (I John 4:19, NKJV). It is important to talk about God's love during the counseling process so that the counselee understands and knows God's love available.

The justice of God is truly clear that He is God of justice, and He is impartial and kind, but His judgment is righteous. "Righteous and justice are the foundation of your throne; steadfast love and faithfulness go before you," (Psalm 89:14, NIV). "For I, the Lord, love justice in the burnt offering…" (Isaiah 61:8, NKJV). "Surely God will never do wickedly, Nor will the Almighty pervert justice," (Job 34:12, NKJV). "He is the Rock, His work is perfect, for all His ways are just; A God of faithfulness and without injustice, Righteous and upright is He," (Deut. 32:4, NKJV). The Justice of God is one of God's attributes. It is important during counseling process to tell the counselee that God is a loving God but He is also God of justice, punishing the children for their parents, "For I, the Lord your God, am a jealous God, visiting the iniquity of the fathers upon the children to the third and fourth generations of those of those who hate Me," (Deut. 5:9, NKJV).

The providence of God is that He is Self-Sufficient, and He is Jehovah Jireh, the provider and sustainer of life. In the counseling process, the importance of God's providence needs to be shared with the counselee that He is omniscient all knowing, omnipotent all powerful, omnipresent always present not limited with space or location. The counselee needs to be encouraged that God is sufficient for every human problem and that He is always willing to engage with anyone who is willing to let Him in, (Rev. 3:20, NKJV). The sovereignty of God is His power, authority, and justice over the universe and that He is omniscience, omnipotent and omnipresent. Therefore, the importance of God's sovereignty to the counseling process is that he is in control of every situation and destiny of the counselee and the counselor. God's right and power rest on Him alone and whatever He decides will come to pass.

God's Command to Politicians

Politicians have put in their positions by God, and they should work for the civil governments for the benefits of the citizens. The politicians should work for God and the people even though they in a secular world. The politicians should be aware to whom they give their allegiance. God only deserves the honor, the praise, worship, and the allegiance. "Blessed is the nation whose God is the Lord, the people He has chosen as His is own. inheritance. The Lord looks from heaven; He sees all the sons of men," (Psalm 33:12-13, NKJV). The politicians can be wicked and cruel towards the people they rule and God is not pleased with such conduct. "When the wicked rise to power, people go into hiding, the righteous thrive," (Proverbs 28:28, NIV). As the Creator of the universe, God is against the rulers who are not compassionate and kind to the populace of their nations. He wants justice to prevail. "When the righteous thrive, the people rejoice; when the wicked rule, the people groan," (Proverbs 29:2, NIV).

The politician should be aware not to fulfill Satan's agenda. Some governments do not give reverence to God. Satan is working in the world against God's agenda using the spiritual forces in the air because he is the prince of the air. Spiritual warfare is real and the Apostle Paul warns and makes us aware that we are not fighting against flesh and blood but against spirituality. "Put on the whole armor of God, that ye may be able to stand against the wiles of the devil. For we do not wrestle against flesh and blood, but against principles, against powers, against the rulers of the darkness of this age, against spiritual hosts of the wickedness in the heavenly places," (Eph. 6:11-12, KJV). The devil is working against the believers, and we have to put the armor of God. "Resist the devil and he will flee from you. "Submit yourselves, therefore to God. Resist the devil, and he will flee from you," (James 4:7, ESV). Saturate your minds with the Holy Scriptures and learn not in your own understanding. "Trust in the Lord with all thine heart;

and lean not unto thine own your understanding. In all thy ways acknowledge him, and he shall direct thy paths," Proverbs 3:5-6, KJV).

Satan is regarded as an angel who rebelled against God and puffed himself up and thought himself to be equal to God. Christian tradition refers to Isaiah 14:12, NKJV, and Ezekiel 28:12-15, NKJV, as referring to Satan. He is viewed as the angel who possessed great piety and beauty but fell with the hosts of angels. His name is the Devil, Satan, the old serpent in the Garden of Eden who influenced Eve and Adam to sin against God (Gen. 3:1-24, NKJV). Satan is the evil spirit who is the god of this world. "In whom the god of this world hath blinded the minds of them which believe not, lest the light of the glorious gospel of Christ, who is the image of God, shine unto them," (II Cor. 4:4, KJV). Satan is the false god of this world. Apostle Paul refers to Satan with his demons as principalities, the powers, the rulers, spiritual hosts in heavenly places (Eph. 6:12-13, KJV).

"And no wonder, for Satan himself masquerades as an angel of light," (II Cor. 11:14, NIV). He comes as an angel of light, but he is wicked, and his schemes are deceptive and corrupt. "When he tells a lie, he speaks from his own nature, because he is a liar and the father of liars," (John 8:44, NKJV). Satan tempted Christ in the wilderness three times, on hedonism - hunger/satisfaction, egoism - specular/might, materialism - kingdoms/wealth (Matt. 4:1-11, NKJV). Be alert and of sober mind. Your enemy the devil prowls around like a roaring lion looking for someone to devour," (I Pet. 5:8, NKJV).

Death is the last enemy to be destroyed. "But it has now been revealed through the appearing of our Savior, Christ Jesus, who has destroyed death and brought life and immortality to light through the gospel, (II Tim. 1:10; Heb. 2:14; I Cor. 15:26, NIV). The devil will cast in the lack of fire. "And the devil, who has deceived them, was thrown into the lake of burning sulfur, where the beast and the false prophet had been thrown. They will be tormented day and night for and ever (Rev. 20:10, NIV). It is also important to note that, Christians are obligated to respect and to honor the government put by God. "Let everyone be subject to the governing authorities, for there is no authority except that which God has established by God. Consequently, whoever rebels against the authority is rebelling against what God has instituted, and those who do so will bring judgment on themselves," (Romans, 13:1-2, NIV). It is noticeably clear that every government in authority has been put by God and all citizens should be submit to its rule. However, if the government violets justice and treat people unfairly, then it is no longer represent God and good governance.

God's Command to Social Justice

God is God of justice and God demands justice for every government to uphold justice and the sanctity of life. God has given humankind the governments to rule with justice and fairness because all human beings are God-image bearers hence, He wants everyone to be treated with dignity, mutual respect and honor. "But let justice run down like waters and righteousness like a mighty stream," (Amos 5:24, NKJV). God's justice is the standard everywhere and He requires fairness and rule of law instituted by the civil society. "Righteousness and justice are the foundation of your throne; Mercy and truth go before your face," (Psalm 89:14, NKKV). God's expectations from humankind are to do three things, "He has shown you, O mortal, what is good. And what does the Lord require of you? To act justly and to love mercy and to walk humbly with your God," (Micah 6:8, NIV). To understand God's mindset about His justice, we must understand and analyze His five attributes to show that He is watching every affair happening in the world because He is sovereign. The six attributes of God are categorized in two main sections, incommunicable attributes of God which are possessed by God alone, not any other which I will list. They are also communicable qualities of God that are possessed by both God and human beings, but not perfectly on the side of man. I will not list those that we resemble God. The six attributes of God:

1. **Infinite**- God's self-existence, without origin, self-sufficient, (Colossians 1:17; Psalm 147:5, NKJV).
2. **Immutable**- God never changes, He is always the same yesterday, today, and forever. He changes not. He executes His plans as they are and He promises are always kept, (Romans 8:35-39, NKJV).
3. **Self-Sufficient**- God does not lack or need anything. He is not limited. He is complete and whole, and He has wisdom, power, authority, and goodness, (John 5:26; Gen. 17:1; Eph. 3:16, NKJV).
4. **Omnipotent**- God is all powerful and majesty. By His word, the heavens were created, (Psalm 33:6; Job 11:7-11; Heb. 6:18, NKJV). He has unlimited power.
5. **Omniscience**- God is all knowing because he remembers the past and the present at the same time. He says, "My purpose will stand, and I will do all that I please," (Isaiah 46:9-10, NIV). "But the very hairs of your head are all numbered. Do not fear; therefore, you are of more value than many sparrows, (Luke 12:7, NKJV).
6. **Omnipresen**t- Everywhere is always in God's presence. "Where shall I go from your Spirit? Or where shall I flee from your presence," (Psalm 139:7, ESV). He is not limited by space or location. He is the Spirit. "Where can I go from your Spirit? Or where can I flee from your presence? If I ascend to heaven, you are there, If I make my bed in Sheol, behold, you are there. If I take the wings of the dawn, if I dwell in the remotest part of the sea, even there in your hand will lead me, and your right hand will lay hold of me." (Psalm 139:7-10; Jeremiah 23:23-24, NIV).

Nothing is hidden in His sight, and He observes everyone and everywhere at the same time. He is not limited to time, space, or location. Those who are on the thrones, governments, institutions, in leadership positions are the custodians of human affairs. They are representatives of God in many ways.

God's Command to Economists

For people to thrive and live happily to fulfill their purposes in lives, the economy of each country must be producing enough products for the nation. The Gross Domestic Product which is the total market value of all final goods and services within a country. The monetary value of all the goods and services make the country to thrive. The sectors such as agriculture, mining, education, industry, health, commerce, technology, tourism, and human resources. The natural resources that God gave to each nation is for the benefit every citizen. The politicians who are in power they usually usurp and become greedy to get involved in corruption and taking the resources to themselves leaving the poor people poorer. As a result, the rich become more richer, and the country may suffer economic slump. Corruption can wreck-havoc in the civil society if the laws of the land cannot protect the poor. Those who are rich need the same protection by the law of the land to do their businesses fairly and freely without any interference from the government if they follow the rules and the laws.

The government's main job is to create a conducive economic environment for gid and small businesses, entrepreneurship, industry, commerce to strive. When the population engages in the economic development, it empowers the citizens to create wealth for themselves, for the society and to the nation at large. It all starts with families who are enabled to invest on their children through solid education as the foundation. Parents count the costs of their children. They start with analyzing cost effectiveness for their children. If their investment on children is not cost effective, that is, after completing their education, do the benefit from the education they offered to their children. If they don't benefit, it means their investment was not cost effective because if the cost exceeds the benefits, then it was not worth investing to the education of the children. However, if the benefits exceed the costs, then it means the investment to their children was cost effective. The cost benefit analysis should help the parents to invest to the scholarships of their children.

Medical Anthropology & Clinical Psychology Summarized

In summary of the subject matter discussed in this book. Medical Anthropology is the study of human health, disease, treatment, prevention, and health care system. This includes the scientific study of humanity, human behavior, human biology, culture, linguistics, and societies, in the past, present, and future. Medical Anthropology investigates and examines people's health and illness in the context of understanding their bodies and souls. Medical Anthropology draws upon social, cultural, biological, and linguistic phenomena. Clinical Psychology, by definition, is the study of the assessment, diagnosis, and treatment of mental illness or mental disorders. Clinical Psychology includes dealing with various mental conditions, including depression, manic depression bipolar disorder, and schizophrenia. Medical anthropology and Clinical Psychology play pivotal roles in human health around the world and in every in all communities.

BIBLIOGRAPHY

Anchin, J. C., & Pincus, A. L. (2010). Evidence-based interpersonal psychotherapy with personality disorders: Theory, components, and strategies. In J. J. Magnavita (Ed.), *Evidence-based treatment of personality dysfunction: Principles, methods, and processes* (113–166).

Good, Bryan J. *Medicine, Rationale and Experience*, New York: University of Cambridge Press, 1994.

Gordon J. Wenham, *Genesis 1-15*, Word Biblical Commentary, vol. 1., Waco, TX: Word, 1987.

Kleinman, Arthur. *Experience and its Moral Modes: Culture and Human Conditions and Disorder*, The Tanner Lectures on Human Value, Stanford University: 1998.

Mattingly, Cheryl. *Moral Laboratories: Family Peril and the Struggle for a Good Life,* Berkeley, CA: University of California Press, 2014.

Mathews, A. Kenneth, *Genesis 1-11:26*, The New American Commentary, vol. 1A Nashville: Broadman & Holman, 1996.

REFERENCES

American Psychiatric Association. (2013). *Diagnostic and statistical manual of mental disorders* (5th ed.). Arlington, VA: American Psychiatric Publishing. Retrieved December 25, 2018, from Walden University Database/ https://class.waldenu.edu

Laureate Education. (Producer). (2012). *Psychopathology: Depressive, bipolar disorders, and suicide.* Retrieved December 25, 2018, from https://class.waldenu.edu.

Tychkov. A.V., Churakov. P.P., Alimuradov. A.K., Tychkova. A. N., and Ageykin. A. V., *New Signal Markers of Borderline Mental Disorders in EEG*, Retrieved December 25, 2018, p. 695. Pare. 3. from https://ieeexplore-ieee- org.ezp.waldenulibrary.org/stamp/stamp.

McCann B., and Landers S. (2010), *Hypnosis in the Treatment of Depression: Considerations in Research Designs and Methods*, HHS Public Access, Apr. (2), 147-164. URL https://www.ncbi. nlm.nih.gov/pmc/articles/PMC2856099.

Yapko MD. *Hypnosis and the treatment of depressions: Strategies for change.* New York: Brunner/ Mazel; 1992. URL https://www.tandfonline.com/doi/abs/10.1080/00029157.1994.10403098.

Syrjala K., Cummings C., and Donaldson G., (1992), *Hypnosis or cognitive behavioral training for the reduction of pain and nausea during cancer treatment: a controlled clinical trial, Vol. 48. Issue 2.* Feb., pp. 137-146. URL https://www.sciencedirect.com/science/article/pii/030439599290049H.

American Psychological Association (Producer). (2009). Session 2 [Video segment]. In *Psychoanalytic Therapy Over Time* (DVD). *Series VIII – Psychotherapy in Six Sessions.* Retrieved January 10, 2019 from Walden Library, Database.

Teyber, E., & Teyber, F. H. (2017). *Interpersonal process in therapy: An integrative model* (7th ed.). Belmont, CA: Brooks/Cole. Retrieved January 15, 2019, from Walden Library database.

American Psychiatric Association. (2013). *Diagnostic and statistical manual of mental disorders* (5th ed.). Arlington, VA: American Psychiatric Publishing, Retrieved December 20, 2018 from Walden Library databases.

Bernal, G., Jimenez-Chafey, M. I., & Domenech-Rodrigues, M. M. (2009). *Cultural adaptations of treatments: A resource for considering culture in evidence-based practice. Professional Psychology: Research and Practice*, 40(4), 361-368. Retrieved December19, 2018, from Walden Library databases, https://ed-ebscohost-com.ezp.waldenulibrary.ord/eds/.

Crosby, J. P., & Sprock, J. (2004). Effect of patient sex, clinician sex, and sex role on the diagnosis of antisocial personality disorder: Models of under-pathologizing and over-pathologizing biases. *Journal of Clinical Psychology, 60*(6), 583–604. Retrieved December 18, from the Walden Library databases.

Paris, J. (2015*). The intelligent clinician's guide to the DSM-5* (2nd ed.). New York, NY: Oxford University Press. Retrieved December 19, 2018, from the Walden Library Databases.

Kaslow, N. J. (2004). Competencies in professional psychology. *American Psychologist, 59*(8), 774–781. Retrieved December 4, 2018, from the Walden Library databases. https://eds-a-ebscohost-com.ezp.waldenulibrary.org/eds/

Laureate Education. (Producer). (2012). *Psychopathology: Substance-related and addictive disorders.* Retrieved December 4, 2019, from https://class.waldenu.edu.

American Psychiatric Association. (2013). *Diagnostic and statistical manual of mental disorders* (5th ed.). Arlington, VA: American Psychiatric Publishing. Retrieved 17, 2019, from Walden Library Database.

American Psychological Association (Producer). (2009). Session 5 [Video segment]. In Psychoanalytic Therapy Over Time (DVD). Series VIII – Psychotherapy in Six Sessions. Retrieved January 17, 2019, from Walden Library Databases.

Bernal, G., Jiménez-Chafey, M. I., & Domenech-Rodrígues, M. M. (2009). Cultural adaptations of treatments: A resource for considering culture in evidence-based practice. *Professional Psychology: Research and Practice, 40*(4), 361–368. Retrieved January 18, 2019 from the Walden Library databases, https://eds-a-ebscohost-com.ezp.waldenulibrary.org/eds/

Burrow-Sanchez, J. J. (2006). Understanding adolescent substance abuse: Prevalence, risk factors, and clinical implications. *Journal of Counseling & Development, 84*(3), 283–290. Retrieved January 17, 2019, from the Walden Library databases.

Escobar, J. I., & Vega, W. A. (2006). Cultural issues and psychiatric diagnosis: Providing a general background for considering substance use diagnoses. *Addiction, 101*(Suppl), 40–47. Retrieved January 16, 2019, from the Walden Library databases.

Gallardo, M. E., Johnson, J., Parham, T. A., & Carter, J. A. (2009). Ethics and multiculturalism: Advancing cultural and clinical responsiveness. *Professional Psychology: Research & Practice, 40*(5), 425-435. Retrieved January 19, 2019, from the Walden Library databases. https://eds-a-ebscohost-com.ezp.waldenulibrary.org/eds/

Kaslow, N. J. (2004). Competencies in professional psychology. *American Psychologist, 59*(8), 774–781. Retrieved January 18, 2019, from the Walden Library databases. https://eds-a-ebscohost-com.ezp.waldenulibrary.org/eds/

Kraemer, W. P. (1958). The dangers of unrecognized countertransference. The Journal of Analytical Psychology, 3(1), 329–341. doi:10.1111/j.1465- 5922.1958. 00029.x Retrieved January 18, 2019 from Walden Library Databases.

Laureate Education. (Producer). (2012). *Psychopathology: Substance-related and addictive disorders.*[Video file]. Retrieved January 18, 2019, from https://class.waldenu.edu

Teyber, E., & Teyber, F. H. (2017). *Interpersonal process in therapy: An integrative model* (7th ed.). Belmont, CA: Brooks/Cole. Retrieved January 19, 2019, from Walden Library Databases.

Bernal, G., Jiménez-Chafey, M. I., & Domenech-Rodrígues, M. M. (2009). Cultural adaptations of treatments: A resource for considering culture in evidence-based practice. *Professional Psychology: Research and Practice, 40*(4), 361–368. Retrieved November 5, 2018 from the Walden Library databases, https://eds-a-ebscohost-com.ezp.waldenulibrary.org/eds/

Gallardo, M. E., Johnson, J., Parham, T. A., & Carter, J. A. (2009). Ethics and multiculturalism: Advancing cultural and clinical responsiveness. *Professional Psychology: Research & Practice, 40*(5), 425-435. Retrieved November 7, 2018, from the Walden Library databases. https://eds-a-ebscohost-com.ezp.waldenulibrary.org/eds/

Kaslow, N. J. (2004). Competencies in professional psychology. *American Psychologist, 59*(8), 774–781. Retrieved October 23, 2018, from the Walden Library databases. https://eds-a-ebscohost-com.ezp.waldenulibrary.org/eds/

Management Sciences for Health. (n.d.). *The provider's guide to quality and culture: Quality and culture quiz.* Retrieved June 1, 2011, from *http://academicdepartments.musc.edu/gme/pdfs/ Quality%20and%20Culture %20Quiz.pdf*

Lithwick, D. Urinalysis: The Supreme Court's torturous justification of high-school urine tests. *Slate.* Retrieved from the Walden Library databases, 2002, July 3.

O'Meara, Kelly Patricia. "Vaccines May Fuel Autism Epidemic; A new study indicates childhood vaccines containing a mercury-based preservative may be the culprits behind the surge in autism cases sweeping the United States." *Insight on the News,* 24 June 2003, p. 24.

Joormann J., Teachman B., and Gotlib I., (2009). *Sadder and Less Accurate? False Memory for Negative Material in Depression*, pp. 412-417. Retrieved October 2, 2018, from https:// waldenulibrary.org/

Githin J., Lythe K., Workman C., Moll J., Zahn R., *European Psychiatry: Early Life Stress Explains Reduced Positive Memory Biases in Remitted Depression.* Elsevier Manson, Vol. 45. Pp. 59-64, September 2017. Retrieved October 2, 2018, from https://www.sciencedirect.com/science/article/.

American Psychiatric Association. (2013). *Diagnostic and statistical manual of mental disorders* (5th ed.). Arlington, VA: American Psychiatric Publishing, Retrieved December 22, 2018, Walden University, Database.

Bernal, G., Jiménez-Chafey, M. I., & Domenech-Rodrígues, M. M. (2009). Cultural adaptations of treatments: A resource for considering culture in evidence-based practice. *Professional Psychology: Research and Practice, 40*(4), 361–368. Retrieved December 21, 2018, from the Walden Library databases, https://eds-a-ebscohost-com.ezp.waldenulibrary.org/eds/

Crosby, J. P., & Sprock, J. (2004). Effect of patient sex, clinician sex, and sex role on the diagnosis of antisocial personality disorder: Models of under pathologizing and over pathologizing biases. Journal of Clinical Psychology, 60(6), 583–604. Retrieved December 22, from the Walden Library databases.

Jovev, M., McKenzie, T., Whittle, S., Simmons, J. G., Allen, N. B., & Chanen, A. M. (2013). Temperament and maltreatment in the emergence of borderline and antisocial personality pathology during early adolescence. Journal of The Canadian Academy of Child & Adolescent Psychiatry, 22(3), 220–229. Retrieved from the Walden Library databases.

Kaslow, N. J. (2004). Competencies in professional psychology. *American Psychologist, 59*(8), 774–781. Retrieved December 21, 2018, from the Walden Library databases. https://eds-a-ebscohost-com.ezp.waldenulibrary.org/eds/

Laureate Education. (Producer). (2012). *Psychopathology: Personality disorders.* [Video file]. Retrieved December 23, 2018, from https://class.waldenu.edu.

Gallardo, M. E., Johnson, J., Parham, T. A., & Carter, J. A. (2009). Ethics and multiculturalism: Advancing cultural and clinical responsiveness. *Professional Psychology: Research & Practice, 40*(5), 425-435. Retrieved December 22, 2018, from the Walden Library databases. https://eds-a-ebscohost-com.ezp.waldenulibrary.org/eds/

Management Sciences for Health. (n.d.). *The provider's guide to quality and culture: Quality and culture quiz.* Retrieved December 22, 2018, 2011 from *http://academicdepartments.musc.edu/ gme/pdfs/Quality%20and%20Culture %20Quiz.pdf*

American Psychological Association (Producer). (2009). In *Psychoanalytic Therapy Over Time (DVD). Series VIII – Psychotherapy in Six Sessions.* Retrieved January 14, 2019, from Walden Library, Database.

American Psychological Association (Producer). (2012). *Interpersonal-relational integrative approach to collaborating with men* [Video file]. Retrieved January 16, 2019 from Psychography database.

Anchin, J. C., & Pincus, A. L. (2010). Evidence-based interpersonal psychotherapy with personality disorders: Theory, components, and strategies. In J. J. Magnavita (Ed.), *Evidence-based treatment of personality dysfunction: Principles, methods, and processes* (pp. 113–166). Washington, DC: American. Psychological Association. doi:10.1037/12130-00, Retrieved January 14, 2019, from the Walden Library databases.

Caligor, E., Kernberg, O.F., & Clarkin, J. F. (2007). *Handbook of dynamic psychotherapy for higher level personality pathology.* Washington, D.C.: American Psychiatric Publishing. Retrieved January 15, 2019, from Walden Database.

Kraemer, W. P. (1958). The dangers of unrecognized countertransference. *The Journal of Analytical Psychology, 3* (1), 329–341. doi:10.1111/j.1465- 5922.1958.00029.x Retrieved January 15, 2019 from the Walden Library databases.

Racker, Hienrich, *Transference and Counter-transference*: Behavioral Sciences, (1ˢᵗ Ed.), London: Routledge. Retrieved January 15, 2019, https://www.taylorfrancis.com/books/9780429908972.

Seth, Messinger, *ANTH 215 A*, Lectures 1, 2, 3, and 4, 22, 29, 31, 2018, p. 8, 9, 17, 21, 33.

American Psychological Association (Producer). (2009). In *Psychoanalytic Therapy Over Time* (– *Psychotherapy in Six Sessions*. Retrieved January 7, 2019, from Walden Library, Database.

American Psychological Association (Producer). (2012). *Interpersonal-relational integrative approach to working with men*. Retrieved January 6, from Psychography database.

Fujii, D. (2002). Neuropsychiatry of Psychosis Secondary to Traumatic Brain Injury. *Psychiatric Times, 19*(8), 33. Retrieved January 10, 2019, from the Walden Library databases.

Safran, J. D., & Muran, J. C. (2000). *Negotiating the therapeutic alliance: A relational treatment guide*. New York, NY: Guilford Press. Retrieved January 8, 2019, from Walden Library Database.

Safran, J. D. (1993). Breaches in the therapeutic alliance: An arena for negotiating authentic relatedness. *Psychotherapy, 30*(1), 11–24. Retrieved January 10, 2019.

Tandon, R. (2013). Schizophrenia and other psychotic disorders in DSM-5. *Clinical Schizophrenia & Related Psychoses, 7*(1), 16–19. Retrieved January 9, 2019, from the Walden Library databases.

Teyber, E., & Teyber, F. H. (2017). *Interpersonal process in therapy: An integrative model* (7ᵗʰ ed.). Belmont, CA: Brooks/Cole. Retrieved January 2, 2019, from Walden Library database.

American Psychological Association (Producer). (2009). In *Psychoanalytic Therapy Over Time* (DVD). *Series VIII – Psychotherapy in Six Sessions*. Retrieved January 14, 2019, from Walden Library, Database.

Bernal, G., Jiménez-Chafey, M. I., & Domenech-Rodrígues, M. M. (2009). Cultural adaptations of treatments: A resource for considering culture in evidence-based practice. *Professional Psychology: Research and Practice, 40*(4), 361–368. Retrieved January 2, 2018 from the Walden Library databases, https://eds-a-ebscohost-com.ezp.waldenulibrary.org/eds/

Burrow-Sanchez, J. J. (2006). Understanding adolescent substance abuse: Prevalence, risk factors, and clinical implications. *Journal of Counseling & Development, 84*(3), 283–290. Retrieved December 3, 2019, from the Walden Library databases.

Escobar, J. I., & Vega, W. A. (2006). Cultural issues and psychiatric diagnosis: Providing a general background for considering substance use diagnoses. *Addiction, 101*(Suppl), 40–47. Retrieved December 3, 2019, from the Walden Library databases.

Gallardo, M. E., Johnson, J., Parham, T. A., & Carter, J. A. (2009). Ethics and multiculturalism: Advancing cultural and clinical responsiveness. *Professional Psychology: Research & Practice, 40*(5), 425-435. Retrieved December 2, 2018, from the Walden Library databases. https://eds-a-ebscohost-com.ezp.waldenulibrary.org/eds/

Kaslow, N. J. (2004). Competencies in professional psychology. *American Psychologist, 59*(8), 774–781. Retrieved December 3, 2018, from the Walden Library databases. https://eds- a-ebscohost-com.ezp.waldenulibrary.org/eds/

Management Sciences for Health. (n.d.). *The provider's guide to quality and culture: Quality and culture quiz.* Retrieved December 2, 2019, from *http://academicdepartments.musc.edu/gme/pdfs/Quality%20and%20Culture %20Quiz.pdf*

Donovan, R. A., & Ponce, A. N. (2009). Identification and measurement of core competencies in professional psychology: Areas for consideration. Training and Education in Professional Psychology, 3(4 Suppl), S46–S49. Retrieved October 24, 2018, from the Walden Library databases. https://eds-a-ebscohost-com.ezp.waldenulibrary.org/

Fouad, N. A., Grus, C. L., Hatcher, R. L., Kaslow, N. J., Hutchings, P. S., Madson, M. B. Crossman, R. E. (2009). Competency benchmarks: A model for understanding and measuring competence in professional psychology across training levels. *Training Education in Professional Psychology, 3*(4, Suppl), S5–S26. Retrieved October 24, 2018, from the Walden Library databases. https://eds-b-ebscohost com.ezp.waldenulibrary.org/eds/

Capuzzi, D., and Stauffer D. M., (2016), (Ed.), *Counseling and Psychotherapy: Theories and Interventions*, American Counseling Association Alexandria: VA.

Kaslow, N. J. (2004). Competencies in professional psychology. *American Psychologist, 59*(8), 774–781. Retrieved October 23, 2018, from the Walden Library databases. https://eds-a- ebscohost-com.ezp.waldenulibrary.org/eds/

American Psychological Association (Producer). (2012). *Interpersonal-relational integrative approach to working with men* [Video file]. Retrieved January 16, 2019 from PsycTHERAPY database.

Anchin, J. C., & Pincus, A. L. (2010). Evidence-based interpersonal psychotherapy with personality disorders: Theory, components, and strategies. In J. J. Magnavita (Ed.), *Evidence-based treatment of personality dysfunction: Principles, methods, and processes* (pp. 113–166).

Washington, DC: American. Psychological Association. doi:10.1037/12130-00, Retrieved January 14, 2019 from the Walden Library databases.

American Psychological Association (Producer). (2012). *Interpersonal-relational integrative approach to working with men* [Video file]. Retrieved January 15, from PsycTHERAPY database.

Richardson, L. F. (1998). Psychogenic dissociation in childhood: The role of the clinical psychologist. *The Counseling Psychologist, 26*(1), 69–100. Retrieved January 14, 2019 from the Walden Library databases.

Safran, J. D., & Muran, J. C. (2000). *Negotiating the therapeutic alliance: A relational treatment guide.* New York, NY: Guilford Press. Retrieved January 14, 2019, from Walden Library Database.

Safran, J. D. (1993). Breaches in the therapeutic alliance: An arena for negotiating authentic relatedness. *Psychotherapy, 30*(1), 11–24. Retrieved January 15, 2019.

Tandon, R. (2013). Schizophrenia and other psychotic disorders in DSM-5. *Clinical Schizophrenia & Related Psychoses, 7*(1), 16–19. Retrieved January 15, 2019, from the Walden Library databases.

Teyber, E., & Teyber, F. H. (2017). *Interpersonal process in therapy: An integrative model* (7th ed.). Belmont, CA: Brooks/Cole. Retrieved January 14, 2019, from Walden Library database.

Paris, J. (2015). *The intelligent clinician's guide to the DSM-5* (2nd ed.). New York, NY: Oxford University Press.

Caligor, E., Kernberg, O.F., & Clarkin, J. F. (2007). *Handbook of dynamic psychotherapy for higher level personality pathology.* Washington, D.C.: American Psychiatric Publishing. Retrieved January 15, 2019, from Walden Database.

Bernal, G., Jiménez-Chafey, M. I., & Domenech-Rodrígues, M. M. (2009). Cultural adaptations of treatments: A resource for considering culture in evidence-based practice. *Professional Psychology: Research and Practice, 40*(4), 361–368. Retrieved November 5, 2018 from the Walden Library databases, https://eds-a-ebscohost-com.ezp.waldenulibrary.org/eds/

Gallardo, M. E., Johnson, J., Parham, T. A., & Carter, J. A. (2009). Ethics and multiculturalism: Advancing cultural and clinical responsiveness. *Professional Psychology: Research & Practice, 40*(5), 425-435. Retrieved November 7, 2018, from the Walden Library databases. https://eds-a-ebscohost-com.ezp.waldenulibrary.org/eds/

Kaslow, N. J. (2004). Competencies in professional psychology. *American Psychologist, 59*(8), 774–781. Retrieved October 23, 2018, from the Walden Library databases. https://eds-a-ebscohost-com.ezp.waldenulibrary.org/eds/

Wikipedia, (n.d.). Retrieved November 6, 2018, from https//en.m. Wikipedia.org/wiki/Slavery in the United States.

Kraemer, W. P. (1958). The dangers of unrecognized countertransference. *The Journal of Analytical Psychology, 3* (1), 329–341. doi:10.1111/j.1465- 5922.1958.00029.x Retrieved January 15, 2019 from the Walden Library databases.

Racker, Hienrich, *Transference and Counter-transference*: Behavioral Sciences, (1st Ed.), London: Routledge. Retrieved January 15, 2019, https://www.taylorfrancis.com/books/9780429908972

Safran, J. D., & Muran, J. C. (2000). *Negotiating the therapeutic alliance: A relational treatment guide.* New York, NY: Guilford Press. Retrieved January 15, 2019, from Walden Library Database.

Safran, J. D. (1993). Breaches in the therapeutic alliance: An arena for negotiating authentic relatedness. *Psychotherapy, 30* (1), 11–24. Retrieved January 13, 2019.

Teyber, E., & Teyber, F. H. (2017). *Interpersonal process in therapy: An integrative model* (7th ed.). Belmont, CA: Brooks/Cole. Retrieved January 15, 2019 from Walden Library database.

American Psychological Association (Producer). (2012). *Interpersonal-relational integrative approach to working with men* [Video file]. Retrieved January 7, 2019, from PsycTHERAPY database. Washington, DC: American Psychological Association. doi:10.1037/12130-00, Retrieved January 10, 2019 from the Walden Library databases.

Caligor, E., Kernberg, O.F., & Clarkin, J. F. (2007). *Handbook of dynamic psychotherapy for higher level personality pathology.* Washington, D.C.: American Psychiatric Publishing. Retrieved January 9, 2019 from Walden Database.

Safran, J. D., & Muran, J. C. (2000). *Negotiating the therapeutic alliance: A relational treatment guide.* New York, NY: Guilford Press. Retrieved January 1, 2019, from Walden Library Database.

Safran, J. D. (1993). Breaches in the therapeutic alliance: An arena for negotiating authentic relatedness. *Psychotherapy, 30*(1), 11–24. Retrieved January 3, 2019.

Teyber, E., & Teyber, F. H. (2017). *Interpersonal process in therapy: An integrative model* (7th ed.). Belmont, CA: Brooks/Cole. Retrieved January 2, 2019, from Walden Library database.

American Psychiatric Association. (2013). *Diagnostic and statistical manual of mental disorders* (5th ed.). Arlington, VA: American Psychiatric Publishing. Retrieved December 3, 2019, from Walden Library Database.

Bernal, G., Jiménez-Chafey, M. I., & Domenech-Rodrígues, M. M. (2009). Cultural adaptations of treatments: A resource for considering culture in evidence-based practice. *Professional Psychology: Research and Practice, 40*(4), 361–368. Retrieved December 2, 2018, from the Walden Library databases, https://eds-a-ebscohost-com.ezp.waldenulibrary.org/eds/

Burrow-Sanchez, J. J. (2006). Understanding adolescent substance abuse: Prevalence, risk factors, and clinical implications. *Journal of Counseling & Development, 84*(3), 283–290. Retrieved December 4, 2019 from the Walden Library databases.

American Psychological Association (Producer). (2009). Session 2 [Video segment]. In *Psychoanalytic Therapy Over Time* (DVD). *Series VIII – Psychotherapy in Six Sessions.* Retrieved January 2, 2019, from Walden Library, Database.

American Psychological Association (Producer). (2012). *Interpersonal-relational integrative approach to working with men* [Video file]. Retrieved January 3, from PsycTHERAPY database.

Safran, J. D., & Muran, J. C. (2000). *Negotiating the therapeutic alliance: A relational treatment guide.* New York, NY: Guilford Press. Retrieved January 1, 2019, from Walden Library Database.

Safran, J. D. (1993). Breaches in the therapeutic alliance: An arena for negotiating authentic relatedness. *Psychotherapy, 30*(1), 11–24. Retrieved January 3, 2019.

Teyber, E., & Teyber, F. H. (2017). *Interpersonal process in therapy: An integrative model* (7ᵗʰ ed.). Belmont, CA: Brooks/Cole. Retrieved January 2, 2019, from Walden Library database.

Escobar, J. I., & Vega, W. A. (2006). Cultural issues and psychiatric diagnosis: Providing a general background for considering substance use diagnoses. *Addiction, 101*(Suppl), 40–47. Retrieved December 4, 2019, from the Walden Library databases.

Gallardo, M. E., Johnson, J., Parham, T. A., & Carter, J. A. (2009). Ethics and multiculturalism: Advancing cultural and clinical responsiveness. *Professional Psychology: Research & Practice, 40*(5), 425-435. Retrieved December 4, 2018, from the Walden Library databases. https:// eds-a-ebscohost-com.ezp.waldenulibrary.org/eds/

https://www.google.com/search?q=humans+evolved+from+apes, (Accessed March 19, 2023).

Printed in the United States
by Baker & Taylor Publisher Services